TALKING
TO YOUR CHILD
ABOUT GOD

The Best Christmas Presents Are Wrapped in Heaven (with Elizabeth
    Heller)
Grandparents Are Made for Hugging (with Elizabeth Heller)
Fathers Are Like Elephants Because They're the Biggest Ones Around
    (But They Still Are Pretty Gentle Underneath)
My Mother Is the Best Gift I Ever Got
Love Is Like a Crayon Because It Comes in All Colors
Just Build the Ark and the Animals Will Come: Children on Bible
    Stories
Growing Up Isn't Hard to Do If You Start Out As a Kid
"Mr. President, Why Don't You Paint Your White House Another
    Color!"
Dear God: Children's Letters to God
Dear God, What Religion Were the Dinosaurs?
The Soul of a Man
The Children's God

TALKING TO YOUR CHILD ABOUT GOD

DAVID HELLER, PH.D.

A PERIGEE BOOK

Grateful acknowledgment is made for permission to reprint from Dear God, *copyright © 1987 by David Heller. Used by permission from Doubleday, a division of Bantam Doubleday Dell Publishing Group, Inc.* The Children's God, *copyright © 1986 by David Heller. Used by permission from University of Chicago Press.*

A Perigee Book
Published by
The Berkley Publishing Group
200 Madison Avenue
New York, NY 10016

Copyright © 1988 by David Heller
New introduction copyright © 1994 by David Heller
First Perigee edition: December 1994
Cover design by Keith Sheridan Associates, Inc.
Cover illustration by Linda Montgomery
All rights reserved. This book, or parts thereof, may not be reproduced in any form without permission.
Published simultaneously in Canada

Library of Congress Cataloging-in-Publication Data

Heller, David.
    Talking to your child about God : a book for families of all faiths /
David Heller.
        p.   cm.
    Originally published: New York : Bantam Books, © 1988.
    ISBN 0-399-52128-3
    1. Children—Religious life.   2. Parents—Religious life.
3. Religious education of children.   I. Title.
[BL625.5.H45   1994]
291.4'4—dc20   94-1896
                                                                        CIP

Printed in the United States of America
1   2   3   4   5   6   7   8   9   10

With love for my parents,
Blanche and Marcus Heller;
for my grandfather,
Samuel Goldman ("Pop"),
who joined God during
the writing of this book,
and for my late grandmother,
Molly Goldman, who taught
me so much about God
when I was a child.

CONTENTS

Introduction   *ix*

PART ONE

LAYING THE GROUNDWORK

1   Your Child's Curiosity About God   *3*

2   Creating a Healthy Spiritual Atmosphere   *11*

3   Knowing Yourself Spiritually   *32*

PART TWO

INTRODUCING YOUR CHILD TO GOD

4   Talking to Your Child: Getting Started   *55*

5   Discussing the Notion of God   *71*

6   Discussing God's Role in the World   *93*

PART THREE

HELPING YOUR CHILD FIND GOD

7 Discussing the Nature and Purpose of
Religion 121

8 Discussing Your Religion: Judaism,
Catholicism, Protestantism, Unaffiliated
Belief in God 142

9 The Interfaith Family: A Special
Phenomenon 180

10 God's Role in the Life of Your Child 201

Index 209

INTRODUCTION

Why does a child need God? It's an understandable question for parents who want to make their children's lives as simple and as uncomplicated as possible. After all, given the invisibility of God, the concept of God is not an easy notion to comprehend. The best response to the question that I have heard comes from Michael, an eight-year-old that I interviewed in conjunction with my other books. When asked about God's role, Michael observed: "God has a lot to do with love. God is kinda like the same as love. That's why He's so important." As Michael suggested, introducing a child to God is a way of developing that child's understanding of love. And that, of course, is as basic a parenting task as there is in life.

Yet there are also other equally compelling reasons that God is crucial for a young person's development. God is not only the Supreme Being, but also a unifying principle that helps us understand where we came from and where we are going. God, and our belief and faith in Him, supplies us with strength to weather life's challenges and setbacks, and it furnishes us with proper humility in relation to our successes. God inspires us to put our lives in perspective and prioritize what really matters, and this guiding influence is as relevant for growing youngsters as it is for grown-ups.

If these reasons weren't sufficiently convincing, then we can also turn to the pragmatics of raising children in today's world for further rationale. In a society suffering from a proliferation of violence in television, movies and videos, and in some cases the real-world environment of youngsters, God becomes even more vital as a countervailing moral force in the socialization of children. God symbolizes values and morality, a sense of order, and above all, a loving, dependable constant in an ever-changing, sometimes chaotic and often bewildering world. A child needs God to help him or her navigate the increasingly rough waters of growing up, and doing so in a happy, healthy and socially-conscious manner.

Talking to Your Child About God is a guide to assist you in teaching your child about the source of all creation, God. This book is intended as an aid in better understanding your own child's inner spirituality, and I hope that it will help you nurture that precious quality as sensitively as possible.

As will be evident, I am a great believer in the majesty and power of a child's inner spirit. In a companion book, *Dear God: Children's Letters to God,* and in my other books such as *The Best Christmas Presents Are Wrapped in Heaven* and *Just Build the Ark and the Animals Will Come*, I have attempted to illustrate the joyful innocence children bring to religious matters. I am also convinced that children have great wisdom and much to teach the rest of us, if only we have patience and appreciate what they have to contribute. I believe that young people help to remind us of our own childlike spirit and our yearning for abiding faith. In this way, the task of teaching children about God has a dual purpose: to educate our youngsters and to deepen our own faith and religious understanding. As we enter into the realm of our children's spirituality, it is as if we turn on a little lamp in the family, and the light from that lamp shines on all of us—child, parents, educators and the greater world at large.

DAVID HELLER, Ph.D.
1994

PART ONE

LAYING THE GROUNDWORK

Your Child's Curiosity About God

"Dear God,
   How do you find a mom and dad for each kid? Do you match them up by their religions, what colors they are, or by cities?
   Or maybe something else very different. Maybe you just use a big lottery.
   I must have won but my friend Billy did not do so good. Please help him.

Love,
Paul
(age 9)"

FROM PERSONAL COLLECTION

"Mommy, where was I before I was born?"

"Why did Grandpa get sick and die? Where did he go?"

"Who makes the flowers?"

"Where does God live?"

What does a parent say to a child about God? How does one reach to the heavens or to formal religion to paint a picture of God for a young son or daughter? Those are the compelling questions that faced one thoughtful couple

I know, Cathy and Michael, as they pondered how to respond to their six-year-old boy, Danny. But for Cathy and Michael, these issues were complicated, even though they were both born Protestant. Michael was raised in a home that did not stress the formal worship of God. Cathy was brought up in a devout family that attended religious services regularly and emphasized the importance of religious traditions. So it was with much concern and anxiety that my friends listened motionless as their child Danny asked out of the blue: "Mommy, Daddy, how can I talk to God?"

Before they were married, Cathy and Michael had talked about their religious beliefs and decided that their love for each other would override their differences. "We'll adjust to whatever comes up—we have each other," Michael had said to Cathy. Now that Danny was growing curious about the world and about God, however, they suddenly felt unprepared. They were not at all certain about what to say to Danny.

While some aspects of Cathy and Michael's dilemma may be related to their specific circumstances, their fundamental challenge is one shared by most parents. The choice of raising a child spiritually is a task that knows no religious distinction. How do two individuals become a mother and a father who can offer a sensible, coherent religious outlook to their child?

Like Cathy and Michael, many parents today find themselves uncomfortable and surprisingly uninformed when it comes to answering their children's questions about God; yet most parents do want their children to know about God. Some also want to renew traditional religious ties without necessarily adhering to the beliefs they consider confining and antiquated. But where to turn for guidance? This book is written for parents who want to foster a spiritual awareness—something very special—in their child. It is also written for those who are confused by circumstances like Cathy and Michael's, or parents who aren't sure of their own spiritual beliefs. The greatest gift you can give to your child is the gift of soul—a set of values and understandings with which to view the world. In the course of this book, you will discover ways to help you make God a meaningful part of your family that will enrich the lives of both you and your child.

Issues that will help you come to terms with your own beliefs and instill a spiritual atmosphere in your home will be discussed. You will learn how to initiate conversations about God with your child and how to understand and respond to your child's budding religious curiosities. As the chapters unfold, you will be supported in talking about your own religious background as well as those of other families you know. Ultimately, you will be able to open up a new means of communication with your child—a level of spiritual exchange that will bring you closer together as parents and child.

That does not mean that the process of talking to your child will always be easy and clear. The notions of God, religion, and indeed your child's own personality, are all too complex for ready-made answers. There is no simple recipe for spiritual nurturing, but there are thoughtful guidelines you can consider in your parenting. This book is not prescriptive, based on the tenets of any particular religion, but practical ideas can make the difference between adequate parenting and a rich, deeper parent-child relationship.

What Is Your Role?

Spiritual development is the growth of a child's view of the world. It is the process by which children form a perspective about their families and themselves, and it represents an important means by which a child learns of the complexity and intimacy of life. Like sexual or cognitive development, spiritual development is a natural process which unfolds spontaneously if a child is supported and encouraged. When it is suppressed or inhibited, however, a child is neither adequately equipped to confront religious questions healthily, nor sufficiently secure to get the most out of life.

A major role as a parent is to guarantee that your child has the opportunity for a rewarding life. And the best way to ensure that your child will have a rich childhood is to foster your child's spiritual growth as well as his or her physical, emotional, and intellectual growth. Shaping a child's spiritual side is accomplished through close communication between parent and child. Nurturing the spirit in your little girl or boy is, in fact, no less crucial than developing the mind and body, and you are the key to this development.

Children are very concerned with basic matters of belief. Most children between the ages of four and twelve do think about God—but *what* do they think? There's a story about the late actor David Niven that was his explanation for the incredible poise and self-confidence he enjoyed. When he was a child, every night at bedtime, he would say the Lord's Prayer and start out with "Our Father, who art a Niven. . . ." He figured that if his last name was the same as God's, then he must be pretty special.

My nephew, Carey, is a three-year-old who loves to remember people by the cars they drive. For example, my brother goes along with "blue car" and my father does too. I am linked with "choo-choo" car, since I live in Boston and ride the mass transit. One day, while I was asking him about God, Carey thought for a minute and seemed to be going through one of his usual reflections. Finally, he smiled as he seemed to reach a conclusion. "God," Carey uttered, "has a red sled with toys on it!"

Though their understandings differ by age, many children want to know: "Who made the flowers?" "Why do people fight?" "Where did I come from?" Though ideas may occasionally differ because of diverse religious backgrounds, many children also wish to know: "How powerful is God?" and "Is God a He or a She?" These universal questions demand answers, and children first look to mom and dad to respond to the important questions in life.

What would you say to your child? Kristen, a thirty-three-year-old Presbyterian mother of two, spoke for many parents when she shared this observation about her parenting experiences.

"I can tell that my eight-year-old and even my five-year-old are thinking a lot," Kristen explained. "There's a lot they don't say. But I can see their little heads working, trying to figure out all kinds of things. Once Kari, that's my eight-year-old, was wondering why people like to be by the ocean so much. I thought that was pretty deep for a child. I sometimes wish that I had a better answer for her. They don't teach you those things in school or in church either."

A parent's role is vital. Since you are the interpreter of your child's significant life experiences and the adviser on his or her difficult questions, you are also your child's most influential guide to religious beliefs, practices, and the spiritual process. It is important to encourage individuality while offering this guidance. The role of guide will require both nurturing and wisdom on the part of you and your spouse. Though your parenting responsibilities may sometimes be complicated, your reward will be remarkably simple: the vision of a lovely child on the way to becoming a fuller human being.

In order to successfully parent your son or daughter regarding spiritual matters, you will need to provide direction without being dictatorial; to ask questions and provide answers with dexterity and ease. You must know when to allow your child to explore and when to set healthy limits. You will need to better understand your child's frustration, hurts, and disillusionment, as well as your youngster's hopes and aspirations.

But it *is* possible to prepare yourself with a thoughtful step-by-step approach to talking about God. First you must know yourself and your spouse and together plan a spiritually enlightened home. I will show you how to get started and how to maintain your child's interest. Discussing a variety of evocative subjects, I will act as your guide to such important topics as what God is like, how God is related to your child's everyday existence, and what God has to do with religion. But *you* will become the expert at talking to your child about your family's own special place in God's world.

Once you have explored these subjects, you will be in a much better position to guide your child's spirituality. Ultimately, *you* are the vital human messenger of the Divine Spirit for your child.

Your Child's Spirit and You

The process of seriously considering your child's spiritual development can help you in other ways. It can lead you to a fuller appreciation of the inherent spirit of children, and can also teach you how to free that spirit in your child.

No parent should lose touch with the curiosity, imagination, spontaneity, and spirit of children. With their innocence, children can remind us of spirituality that is simple, straightforward, and incredibly original! For example, one young girl I interviewed, a bright ten-year-old, thought that "heaven might be in California or somewhere." When I asked what the earthquakes were for, she looked puzzled for a minute. Then she finally exclaimed, "Well no place is perfect!"

Asked why the Jewish holiday is called Passover, eleven-year-old Jason explained, "God was at dinner and when He was given some bread, He said, 'No thanks, I will have some matzoh instead.' So he passed over the bread and went for the matzoh. That's how it all started." So you're probably in for a lot of treats when your child explains spiritual matters to you! With their goodness, children can remind us of essential beliefs and values. If nurtured carefully, they will demonstrate a sense of optimism that can rekindle a parent's own faith in God.

A child's spirit is spontaneous and unique. Sitting behind their little desks or kneeling alongside their beds, they may share this spirit with you and tell you just how they see the world. Often they may thank God for good things or ask God questions. But children are conspicuously honest. They may not be shy about voicing a complaint or two.

"About all those wars, Mr. God, what's the story?" one seven-year-old asks. "Why did Grandma die, God?" a nine-year-old schoolmate questions. For children, no one is beyond questioning and that includes God too. Such questions represent a perfect opportunity for a parent to become more familiar with the spirit of a child.

As you speak with your child using the guidelines we will discuss, you will begin to see the emergence of that spirit and will want to cultivate its growth. The better equipped you are to respond to your child's spirituality, the more it will be developed in a way that will endure and enhance the quality of your child's life.

Thus, you are now about to do something very important for your child. You are going to bolster your child's inner spirit, and in doing so, you will also be benefiting yourself and others. For your child, like all children, has a contribution to make to society, and you are the guiding light behind that contribution.

2

Creating a Healthy Spiritual Atmosphere

"Dear God,
   My family, the Sandersons, is pleased to invite your family, the Gods, over for bread and wine (I figured you might like this). You are hereby invited on November the 3, at 7 pm. Please respond in writing or on a tablet by this date.

Very truly yours,
Sheila Sanderson
(age 11)"
FROM *DEAR GOD*

Spirituality in the home is best maintained through an involved and caring parent-child relationship. Being there for your youngster on a deep psychological level and on an everyday caretaking level makes all the difference in the world when it comes to spiritual matters and God.

Fundamental to being there is providing the right kind of atmosphere for your child. Fortunately, we can uncover some definite building blocks to a healthy environment and a spiritually rich relationship among family members. These are essential family characteristics that you can think over and work on with your spouse. They are subjects for meaningful discussion, first between husband and wife, and then later, sources of spiritual sustenance between parent and child.

Expressing Love in the Context of Religion

While most parents understand the unequivocal place of love in the family and believe in raising their children with some form of religious belief, not everyone is aware of the possible relationship between love and religious ideas. But spirituality in your family and home is not possible without love. Without the presence of love, the qualities of trust, freedom, and involvement lose their spiritual meaning. Talking to your child about God without love is like speaking lyrics without a melody. No matter how intelligent or pertinent the words, there will be no song for you to share.

In routine matters or in matters of faith, love is at the core of the parent-child relationship. To bring about a spiritual awareness in your family, it is important to express love in the context of religious beliefs. Whether you rely most heavily on the tenets of formal religion or on your own personal precepts, that mandate applies. Even in a family that follows an established religion with great dedication, religious belief will die if it is separated from its life force—the love that allows parents and children alike to flourish. Until love is integrated with religious ideas, it is difficult for a person or family to discover anything but a very distant God.

So it is important to paint a portrait of a loving God for

your child if that's what you believe in. Consider how God expresses love in many ways (such as providing hope for people who are frightened, and healing for people who are sick or injured). You might draw parallels between your love for your child and God's love. Always keep in mind how God's love might be naturally applicable to the everyday life of your child. For example, God keeps us safe when we play and watches over us when we sleep. He gives us friends to have fun with and parents to care for us.

Unfortunately, sometimes formal religion and love are seen by parents as unrelated or as opposite practices. Religion is often viewed as solemn, pragmatic, and perhaps overbearing. On the other hand, love is pictured as being romantic and idealistic, mostly due to the images presented in literature and popular culture. Because of this contrast, people find the integration of religion and love a very difficult concept. The two subjects just don't seem to belong together if we see the world in this segregated way.

As a parent, you must answer the question: What does religion have to do with love? That is a question pertinent to families of all backgrounds and circumstances, and to children of all ages. It is clearly a subject relevant to the development of all children, from the inquisitive four-year-old to the more worldly and knowledgeable ten-year-old.

Barbara is a Catholic, a mother of four who knows just how important the topic of love and religion is: "Love is probably both the hardest and easiest thing for a parent," Barbara says paradoxically. "What makes it so hard, especially with religion, is that it's difficult to put in words. The Bible is not very explicit about love, either. But when you can put aside your worries you can say to your child: 'God is good and God loves you. . . . And so do I.' It seems so simple, but it's those simple truths about religion that stick with children. They did for my kids."

As Barbara suggests, it *is* possible to talk to your child about how love is an inherent part of formal religion.

You should carry out all religious rituals and activities with love—and you need to feel comfortable expressing that love openly. Candlelighting is just candlelighting if it's an isolated practice; but performed in the spirit of love, it is something very different. Wine is merely an alcoholic beverage if consumed without symbolic significance; but if consumed with love and meaning, it becomes an altogether different experience. Talk to your child about the reasons behind your practices, but most importantly, remember to say how you feel inside while you perform them. Use religious and family rituals to express your love for your child: at prayer before meals; at bedtime prayer; at church or synagogue; on holidays like Easter and Passover.

Lastly, it is your daily affection and positive regard that matters above all; never forget that. Religion is not just a matter of pomp and ceremony. In your home, religion is the spiritual atmosphere that you create through your everyday parenting. You may attend formal religious services every week, but your spiritual life is experienced each and every moment. If love flows comfortably through the center of family life, and is not just an occasional family guest, then belief in a personal God is more likely to become a present reality.

As you begin to consider what you'll actually say to your child about God, remember to bring love into your conversations. Your job as a parent demands that you assure a positive home climate; that is not an easy task. But keep in mind that your home does not have to be perfect, but merely a lively and comfortable place where your child can explore new ideas with reasonable optimism and security.

Remember that children often take things literally; and, just when you think they understand what you've taught them, it turns out that what *they've* just learned may be very different. For example, one of the first Bible passages Michelle learned as a young child was the Twenty-third Psalm. Instead of finding it comforting and assuring, she was terrified by the verse that says, "Surely goodness and mercy shall follow me all the days of my life, and I shall dwell in the House of the Lord forever." Having memorized the psalm before she could read, she was sure that Shirley Goodness and her friend, Mercy, were two old, shrunken women who were going to follow her around for the rest of her life, keeping close track of everything she did wrong. It's small wonder that it took Michelle a long time to think that God was more than a disciplinarian with a full-time crew of spies. A far cry from the loving God she was hearing about. So be careful to clarify with your child exactly what he thinks you've told him.

Establishing Trust With Your Child

Along with love and care, there is absolutely no substitute for basic trust between parent and child. If you want your child to take what you have to offer concerning God seriously, you must instill trust in him or her. No child can find God if he or she feels unsafe in the world. A child needs to feel secure enough to explore, since childhood exploration is the initial meeting place between an individual and God. While the trust that your child develops in you is fundamental, the sense of trust must also transfer to the outside world. Only when your child feels safe enough to take risks at home will he or she feel safe—and bold enough to explore the outside world.

What is this trust that psychologists often speak so freely of? Trust implies a reasonably set and secure environment which is based on consistent principles. But in its spiritual connotation, trust also means that the atmosphere is good for the child and is based on benign principles. That is the ideal kind of atmosphere to create for your child and for the whole family.

The seeds of trust stem from the parent-child interaction which starts at birth, and in our culture, has typically been a mother-child interaction. That's the quintessential notion brought to light by developmental researcher Erik Erikson, in his widely acclaimed work *Childhood and Society* (1963).

In discussing the stages of life, Erikson declares that a trust/mistrust stage is the crucial foundation for all stages of childhood. Erikson's ground-breaking interviews with children revealed that some children show a rudimentary security about their mothers as a fixed object in their lives; other children do not. For those children who are saddled with mistrust, a psychological scar develops which is nearly impossible to remedy. Unable to trust in any enduring way, these children will encounter difficulty later in life when they alone are responsible for autonomy, initiative, and endeavors to form relationships. Individuals with basic trust, on the other hand, are in a better position to thrive in these areas.

What is less well known is that Erikson also speculated that trust was related to religious belief. He believed that the greater the childhood trust of a person, the more optimistic that person would be and the more likely they would be to believe in God. It is a hard thing to prove scientifically, but it makes sense that trust would be central to religious ideas. The importance of trust is implied in the Old Testament, and it is pivotal for most of the great religions. Faith in God is fundamentally a matter of trust in what cannot be seen but what may be realized. We all rely on a certain amount of trust when we profess belief in God.

This sense of trust, tested and challenged by a person's life experiences, is not a quality of the infant or the preschool child alone. As Erikson suggested, trust is a lifelong quality. Trust remains with a person, helping in large part to shape an individual's image of God. In fact, it is the solid base on which a person stands spiritually—and it is from that vantage point that your child, or any person, can comfortably confront the world and its frequently enigmatic questions.

"I have always tried to say to my kids to have faith in things, to believe that everything works out in time," says thirty-eight-year-old Betty, a Catholic mother of three. "When my oldest child's friend moved to a different state, I told her to trust that her friend would keep in contact. It's been four years, and they still write to each other every week. My kids have learned to trust in other people and in their parents too. I think they will always."

But when trust is weak and fragile, a child does not have much inner strength to rely upon. It is difficult to believe in people or in God. Children who largely lack trust are easy to recognize. They encounter interpersonal diffi-

culties and severe adjustment problems in new environ-
ments. Their religious imagery is markedly different too, as
the element of mistrust is discernible in their notions and
pictures of God. Such is the case right now for eight-year-
old Deron, a child of divorced Protestant parents. Deron
rarely sees his father and argues constantly with his mother,
with whom he lives.

"I'm not sure there's any God guy," Deron openly dis-
closes. "If there is, I wouldn't count on Him too much.
There's a lot of bad dudes in the world, making war and
selling drugs. Why does He let that go? Must be He helps
who He wants to help. I can take care of myself. I don't
need religious help," Deron concludes with an abrupt turn-
ing away.

Sadly, Deron's comments reveal his need to trust at the
same time they demonstrate his inability to trust. That is
the sign of a child who did not learn and incorporate basic
trust in infancy.

Fortunately, most children begin with greater trust
than Deron, so trust in God is easier for them to develop.
Religious trust can be developed or discouraged, depending
on the way parents communicate and act as their children
grow. But there are specific means by which religious trust
or mistrust is influenced by parents. The lack of healthy
responses to your youngster's feelings can breed a sense of
mistrust. That mistrust may not be openly voiced by your
youngster, but it will continue to fester into his or her older
years and discolor adult religious ideas. Even if your child
is a preschooler you can begin building a trusting relationship with him or her around God and religion. Pay attention to your own natural instincts, and most of all, believe
in the strength and goodness of your child. Trust is conta-

gious and will spread to other aspects of your family life. Trust is fostered with considerable diligence and effort; mistrust is caused rather easily by inattention and thoughtlessness. How can a parent enhance trust about religion? You can generally build it by empathizing with your child's point of view. Remember that at first, most children find religious ideas to be a bit heavy and foreign, but they *are* fascinated by the notion of God.

Depending on your personal style, and your child's age, there are many specific things you can do to make the worship of God palatable and enjoyable while bolstering trust. Here is a list of ideas that can help you build trust by demonstrating that you are someone who cares and understands your child's spiritual needs.

Ways to Enhance Religious Trust

FOUR- TO SIX-YEAR-OLDS

1. Allow your child to leaf through a favorite prayer book or to hold a religious item and explain its importance.
2. Encourage questions about why you celebrate the holidays that you do (e.g., Easter, Passover).
3. Ask your youngster for suggestions to celebrate a religious holiday. What would he or she especially like to do?
4. Give your child simple picture books on your religion. Tell your child that he or she can either look through the books, or have you read from them.

SEVEN- TO NINE-YEAR-OLDS

1. Encourage your child to get to know youngsters of different religions. Explain how this helps in being accept-

ing of people who are different, and understanding other religions better.

2. If your child currently attends religious school, encourage him or her to openly express opinions about religious questions and issues (e.g., How does confession help a person?).

3. Be careful not to overtly or subtly discourage your child's budding ideas about religion, even if they seem far-fetched to you. Respect your child as an individual. If you wish to present alternatives to your child, do so in a loving and open-ended way. Express, but don't force your religious ideas on your child.

4. Ask your child if he can imagine how God might be involved in the things that interest him (e.g., sports, music).

TEN- TO TWELVE-YEAR-OLDS

1. Explain why you observe religious practices that directly affect your child (e.g., saying grace before meals; fasting on a holiday). Then tell him why you think other people may not observe them.

2. Encourage particularly critical or investigative questions about hard-to-explain events (e.g., Why did Jesus have to die so painfully? Why were six million Jews killed during World War II?).

3. Take your child to a bookstore, and buy a book of his or her choice that pertains to religion or spirituality, and is especially written for his or her age group.

Cultivating Freedom

The concept of religious freedom usually makes us think of colonial settlers or revolutions, but religious freedom is far more than a long-standing historical ideal. It is in fact an important part of an individual's appreciation of God. Any person, adult or child, needs to feel that religious beliefs are freely chosen and genuinely felt. That is when God truly becomes a part of their inner lives.

The fact that religious freedom is a personal and interpersonal phenomenon has obvious relevance for you and your child. What you communicate about freedom will influence whether your child has the opportunity to develop his or her own ideas, as well as heed your views. Cultivating religious freedom in your child will emancipate him from the risk of thoughtless adherence to creeds that have no personal importance. Too many people—both children and adults—recite words or "beliefs" that actually mean very little to them. When this happens, one is closer to being a puppet than a thinking, acting, responsible person. Give your child the green light to search for a living God who is involved in human affairs, and you will avoid the "puppet trap" and earn your son or daughter's respect.

Freedom is thus a prevailing quality of a spiritual home. You can think of religious freedom simply as the atmosphere necessary for the flowering of childhood curiosity. Freedom is a characteristic of an environment which guarantees your child the uninhibited expression of spiritual ideas, questions, and doubts. When you consider your own family, bear in mind that there are always two sides to freedom. As a parent, you must realize that too little or too much freedom is not a good thing. However, steering your youngster between the two is not always a clear-cut task.

Your child, like all youngsters, is born with an inclination to try new things—first the concrete objects of the world (e.g., colored cereal). Later, your child will discover the more abstract pursuits of early adolescent life, such as loud music. As a parent, no matter what the subject of your child's interests, you must strike a balance between parental involvement and passive oversight. Whether curiosity centers around a toy, a warm blanket, or a hot stove, a parent must actively assess the situation. What are the dangers? What will your child learn? The same concerns apply to spirituality and more intangible subjects as you supervise your child's search for answers. Without a parent acting as a kind of human compass, a child is likely to become either painfully uncontrolled or too inhibited.

If a child is uncontrolled, he or she may find it hard to sit still and focus on any single topic. He may form many important spiritual questions but won't be able to pursue answers with any depth. It will also be hard for him to form a coherent image of God. For example, if a child is taught that all behaviors and ideas are acceptable and no limits are placed, then the basic tenets of a formal religion or even a parent's personal ideas are not likely to be adopted. It will also be a problem for the child to settle on his or her own beliefs and practices, preferring instead to live in pursuit of the next new and eye-catching notion—be it spiritual or material. The uncontained child shops for new ideas and needs constant stimulation, like a wayward consumer who can't be satisfied.

Trevor, age thirty-three and a Unitarian father of two, reflects on his own experiences during his early and teenage years.

"When I was growing up," Trevor says, "my parents were overly liberal to the point of not giving us any major thing to believe in. They didn't give us that much direction. In my teens and till I was about twenty-four, I was trying out one religion after another like they were different flavors of ice cream. For a while, I was curious about Jesus, then Buddhists—but they too still seemed too conventional. I even got curious about some small sects. I just couldn't center. I went through a lot before I could settle into any church. Having a family has been a big factor too," Trevor observed in conclusion.

In contrast to the kind of childhood that Trevor describes, some boys and girls are needlessly repressed by their parents. Authoritarian and demanding, rather than guiding and supportive, such parents forbid a child to question religious notions or investigate any outside religious beliefs. The child may grow up fearful of thinking for himself or herself, in addition to living with worry about and suppression of any desire for independence. Such a youngster will be overly tentative about religious ideas, or alternatively, falsely ardent and parrotlike in supporting his or her parents' religious ideas. The constrained child is extremely frustrated underneath, for parents have not adequately respected the individuality of the child. Believing that they know what is best for the youngster, and also feeling that they understand God's will, these parents inhibit a child from a genuine search for God.

Ben, an eight-year-old Baptist child, is a boy who is overly constrained by his parents. When I engaged Ben in structured play, he arranged a set of family dolls. His thoughts about religion and his family were evident; mother doll and father doll were actively portrayed by Ben, while a little boy doll reacted like a marionette. Here is Ben's description of the doll family's exchange about God and religion. It's obvious that the doll family serves as a miniature replica of Ben's real family, and that Ben suffers from a lack of religious freedom.

(Mother and father dolls stand erect, hovering over a little boy doll. The little boy doll is sitting on a small seat, looking downward.)

Ben: "This boy's name is Ken. Here is his mom and the dad. The mom and dad tell Ken to listen to them more about school and about church. They say: 'We know what God wants. You must obey.' Ken listens to them. He has to. Otherwise he will get in trouble. Ken lives real far away from here."

Without religious freedom in the parent-child relationship, a youngster like Ben cannot feel free to pose genuine questions about religion and try to find answers that work for him. That's a shame for certain, because the child will not be able to reach his or her full potential without going through a good deal of rebellion and anguish.

Your challenge as a parent is neither to overconstrain nor to allow your child to roam without direction. Your task is to cultivate a spirit of freedom by combining guidance with tolerance. You must bring these together into an affectionate and intelligent parental package.

Consider bringing about an ambience of openness to your child's questions through a variety of thoughtful steps. Depending on your preferences, you may want to discuss religion with your child while you are engaged in "let-loose" leisure activities: while walking the dog or during a family trip, for example. That may help you to avoid being dogmatic and overly solemn. You may also choose to make your conversations about God and religion lighthearted, casual, and humorous. Humor is a wonderful way to relieve tension and alleviate anxiety when it comes to complicated matters like faith. It also has a way of sanctioning free expression of ideas. Often, your *child* will introduce the humor—unintentionally. Here's one of my favorite accounts of the Red Sea episode in Exodus, as told by eight-year-old Elisa: "It was a real pretty day out and the Jews wanted to get across the sea so that they could play at the beach. They were carrying a lot of heavy stuff, like beach chairs and volleyball nets. The other people were trying to help get them across with their chariots. But they could not find a yacht anywhere. So God helped. He gave the sea a big push so the Jews would get tans and relax!"

There are also ways to encourage freedom that are more central to religious beliefs and practices. You can acknowledge that no person, adult or child, has all the answers about God. "Everyone is free to form their own beliefs," you can explain to your youngster, "but there are ways to learn things about God that can help you decide what you believe." You might also consider saying that many people can have the truth about God, even if their ideas appear at first glance to be in conflict. "Perhaps God respects all our differences," you might suggest to an older child. "The important thing is to love God." That is an excellent way to enter into a discussion of God's attitude toward freedom. What does your child think God's views on religious freedom are? Find out together and you will already be sharing a family experience that celebrates the notion of religious freedom—the right to openly discuss each of your ideas about God.

There are many other ways to foster religious freedom. You can talk about other religions, the history of religious oppression in some countries, the right to perform or abstain from rituals, the right to choose a place of worship—or to decline. The *most* important thing is to make it clear to your child that religious freedom exists here and now—and in your home. In your discussion with your child about religious freedom, show your youngster that you care about what he or she has to say. Demonstrate to your child that you will not pass judgment on his or her ideas, or on your child as a person, by accepting and taking seriously your child's viewpoints. Let him see that you're listening and reacting spontaneously by responding to his views as well as expressing your own. You will not only be cultivating religious freedom but you will also be nurturing and sustaining a loving sense of mutual respect.

Get Involved in Your Child's Life

What does it mean for a parent to be involved? How you resolve that question is another pivotal factor in the creation of a healthy spiritual household. Your involvement is essential for a child to form a rich character and develop sincere interests in spirituality. It will inspire a child to become very involved in the world of ideas and other people.

Involvement implies investment. In order to create a spiritual climate, you must invest in your child. You must invest time, energy, caring, and personal disclosure; you must give of yourself. Without that giving, no amount of parental interest in spirituality is sufficient. You can demonstrate involvement through the considerate, attentive way that you listen to your child. Whether the prevailing issue is an incident at school or a lively narration about his afterschool activities, your child very much requires your undivided interest. Listening means that you need to take time out from your other activities.

The other major way to become involved is to actively bring religion and faith into your home. The best way to do that is to introduce your views to your child. Tell your child about your belief in God and about what that means to you. The more comfortable you feel sharing your beliefs with your child, the closer your son or daughter will feel to you in regard to religion. Your child will view you as more involved if you voice your ideas and will be more inclined to let you in on his or hers as well. Openness about religion has a way of breeding togetherness in families. You can also be actively involved by making books and religious items available which relate to both your beliefs and other religions. That can include the Bible, storybooks, coloring books, video tapes, and music, as well as other sources. Those additions to your home will create a climate that will foster your child's spiritual growth.

The nature of your involvement can correspond to the age and maturation of your child. For the four- to six-year-old child, parents can spend a good deal of playtime talking about a whole variety of subjects, including God and religion. With these youngest children, you can be involved by being an astute listener. Listen closely when your child asks a serious question, like about babies or about animals. That's a good time to offer a bit of simple philosophy about God (e.g., "God is responsible for making animals too.").

For older children, one-to-one time is a necessary way for a parent to get involved. Seven- to nine-year-olds need a parent who is democratic with them about religious ideas and is willing to engage in an open exchange. At the same time, they will expect that you have formed some very definite ideas about God and they'll be eager to hear about them. Get involved by explaining how you see God and then ask your youngster for his or her opinion. Ten- to twelve-year-olds, having already digested your approach to religion, want you to respect them as individuals. Even with these youngsters, individualized attention to their notions about God and people is highly recommended. By asking them questions about their ideas about God and other issues, you can show that your concern for them is consistent in all areas of their lives, not just in their spiritual lives. Such conversations between you and your child will plant the seeds for a healthy adult parent-child relationship years later.

While the best way to increase involvement is through a one-to-one relationship with your child, you and your spouse can get involved further by monitoring other outside influences in your child's life, no matter what his or her age. By monitoring, I mean keeping abreast of your child's interests and acting as a sounding board. Other than through their parents, children develop their religious beliefs through church and formal religious teaching, schools, friends, and the media.

Become involved by finding out what your child thinks about church, synagogue, or other religious institutions. Show that what your youngster feels matters a great deal to you. Ask him which aspects of formal religion have the greatest appeal, and encourage him to discuss any ideas or practices which confuse, frighten, or repel him. Even if your youngster is not fully prepared to divulge all of these feelings, he will know that you are there for him, ready to talk when the timing is right.

Ask your child about whether religion or God is ever

discussed at school or with friends. What are your child's friends' religions? What does your child learn from them or say to them? Is religion ever mentioned in class? With these questions in particular, you will need to balance your interest with circumspection. As much as you want to be close to your child, you don't want to intrude on his or her privacy. So test out an occasional question about school and friends, then interject a comment or two about God or religion, if it's appropriate. It's not the details of your talk that will be most influential, but rather the receptive, nonjudgmental spirit that you display when you discuss your child's life outside the home. This will encourage him or her to feel free to come to you with *whatever* is on his mind.

Media depictions of God and supernatural characters are another strong influence on your child's religious ideas. Get involved by discovering what fictitious characters have captured your child's imagination and how your child sees such a figure in relation to the God you speak about. In other words, does your child group the colorful characters depicted by Saturday morning cartoons in the same category as Joseph, Moses, or John the Baptist? Or does your child see the clear difference? Which images are most compelling for him or her, those from popular culture or the ones from the Bible?

In my interviews with children of different religions, I have found that television and the media play a formidable role in the formation of some children's ideas about God. Popular culture can profoundly shape a child's heroic ideals, major values, and fantasies. Much national attention has been devoted to the effects of television on psychological qualities like aggression, but the impact of television on religious beliefs may be no less powerful.

Ten-year-old Scott, a Baptist youngster, sets a scene of God versus evil as he relates a religious story. Scott claims that God is like "the good guy stars of *Spenser: For Hire*," the television crime-fighting series. Later, Scott comments that conversations with God can be quite unusual, "like when God talked to Moses through a burning bush in [the movie] *The Ten Commandments*." They can also play a central role in the development of doubt and religious tension. As Scott skeptically concludes, "God might be just as unreal as Hercules or Superman."

Scott's ideas are obviously very media-influenced. While your youngster may not be quite as affected by popular culture, you should be aware of the popular notions that matter to your child. Ask, "Who are your favorite heroes and heroines on TV? In the Bible?" Then ask why those figures have such appeal.

Children are often influenced by popular television representations of God rather than the images that come from formal religion or personal concepts. Given how visual the contemporary world has become, children are more prone to imagine figures of God that resemble people—familiar and human gods, surrogate figures who star in a television show or who are cartoon characters. Because these popular depictions of God are accessible and not risky, children often rely on them—particularly during periods of anxiety, confusion, or family turmoil.

Guard against the formation of a facile notion of God. Try to fill your child's world with reading and television that is positive and life-enhancing. Good parenting is a matter of discussing values with your child and considering all influences, whether ideas from popular culture, from formal religion, from parents or from friends. Your involvement will give your child the strength to choose his or her own beliefs, and eventually to create his or her own picture of God.

John, age fifty-five and a Catholic father of four, is vehement about a parent's involvement and offers advice for younger parents. "If I were starting out as a parent today, I'd make sure I knew what my kids were watching and what they thought of it. You can't be looking over their shoulders all the time, but you have to take the time to figure out where they are. I mean the media pretty much elects a president these days, so you have to be careful that television isn't the only way your children learn about God."

The overriding thing to remember is to become involved and remain accessible to your child. No other institution can compensate for an absent parent; no other influence can compete with a sensitive and available parent.

⟨⟩ 3

Knowing Yourself Spiritually

"Dear God,
    My dad thinks he is you. Please straighten him out.

                                    Wayne
                                    (age 11)"
                                    FROM *DEAR GOD*

"Know thyself"—it's a benevolent and wise mandate that priests and philosophers have advocated from time immemorial. The great religious works—the Bible, the Koran, and I Ching—continuously address the topic of self-knowledge in stories and sayings. But it is not just an ancient or esoteric view of life, it is a modern and pragmatic notion. This timeless advice provides you with the opportunity to master a great variety of circumstances, no matter how challenging they may appear.

To relate to a child as a fully spiritual human being, parents must first think of their spiritual awareness. That means believing in a soul or a spiritual dimension, or accepting that there is more to your life than your everyday existence. You may be well on your way already, but a systematic review of your spiritual life can only enhance your understanding of your parental responsibilities. It can also help you grow enormously as a person, and that in turn can also benefit your child. If in this process your own ideas become better defined and your own faith becomes more certain, then your task will be doubly successful.

Such a realization on your part will inevitably benefit your child.

But why else is self-awareness vital for a parent? Knowing yourself allows you to explain to your child what you really believe and why you believe it. It permits you to talk with relative ease about past and current experiences, as well as future expectations which require faith in God. The aim of The Know Yourself Inventory below is to help you organize your spiritual ideas so that you will be prepared when your child makes inquiries or when you initiate conversation with your child.

Set aside at least an hour to take the interview and think about your responses. Each parent should complete the questions separately. However, comparing responses afterward will probably trigger a lively discussion. Most of all, try as best you can to be honest with yourself about what you really believe and what you truly feel. If you are genuine in your convictions, that sincerity will carry over naturally to your conversations with your child.

The Know Yourself Inventory

1. How would you describe your image of God, if you have one? What positive qualities stand out? Are there any negative aspects to the image?

2. List five of your most deeply felt beliefs about God.

3. Has your image of God changed since you were a child?

4. Is formal religion an important part of your life? What beliefs or events substantiate your response?

5. Do you believe life has meaning? If so, what do you believe to be the purpose of your life?

6. Do you believe life is fair and just? What specific events come to mind as you consider your answer?

7. Do you ever think about death? What comes to mind when you think about death?

8. Do you believe in an afterlife or in multiple lifetimes? If so, what do you picture?

9. Do you believe in a negative spiritual force that opposes the will of God? Have you seen evidence of that force in your own life?

10. How, if at all, is God involved in your everyday affairs? How do you best communicate with God?

11. Can you recall a time of your life or an event during which you believed particularly strongly in the existence of God? What was it like?

12. Can you recall a time of your life or an event during which you strongly doubted the existence of God? What was it like?

13. Can you recall a time when you felt especially fearful of God? What were you afraid of? Are you still fearful?

14. Can you recall a period when you felt unusually angry at God? What were you angry about? Does it persist or are there new sources of anger?

15. What things related to religion make you feel guilty? Do you feel that guilt is justified?

16. What would you most like to convey to your child about God?
17. Do you believe that children are born with God in them or do you think they have to be taught about God for the most part?
18. How often do you talk with your spouse about religion? Who usually initiates the conversation? What do you talk about?
19. How do your religious views differ from those of your parents?
20. What spiritual qualities would you like your child to express when he or she is an adult?
21. What would you say to your child if he or she asked, "What matters most in the world?"
22. How do you think you could bring God more into your life?
23. What do you wish God would change about the world?
24. In what ways, if any, is parenting a spiritual experience for you?
25. How does being a parent fit into your overall spiritual development?

As your child turns twelve or thirteen, you may notice the beginnings of an adolescent's skepticism. What was it like for you at that age? You may be surprised and even a bit chagrined by what you recall! One young mother that I spoke with reveals that, as a thirteen-year-old, she thought God would probably leave her alone until she went to college. Then she thought God would reemerge and tell her what career to pursue!

Knowledge about yourself needs to be accessible for you to respond to the curious and sometimes difficult questions your child may pose. Knowledge about your beliefs can avert confusion about religious dogma and rituals. Ultimately, self-knowledge will make you more flexible psychologically, so that you can better understand your visceral reactions to your child's comments and questions. If your child's question, "How do you *know* there's a God?" immediately makes you feel defensive, perhaps you'll know *why* that's true, and you'll be able to overcome the temptation to *respond* defensively.

What do we mean when we say, "know yourself"? No two definitions of self-awareness are identical. Consider these two descriptions from mothers of similar background.

"You have to be comfortable with yourself to be a mother," begins thirty-three-year-old Jenny, a Catholic mother of two. "To talk about religion, you should read about religion. You start by finding meaning in your own life. That should be there before you have kids. Then you can pass it on to your kids, by saying this is how *you* found it to be . . ."

Carol, also a thirty-three-year-old Catholic mother, offers a contrasting view of self-understanding. "I don't buy a lot of psychologizing when it comes to God. I don't try to think things out a lot. I know what I believe. I try to teach my kids through actions. If they have a question, I take time out to answer it of course." Then Carol concluded, "My seven-year-old once asked me, 'Did you go to church when you were my age?' I told her I did, but what's important is that I still go now."

While Jenny stresses the teaching aspects of parenthood, Carol seems to be saying that a parent is most important as a role model for a child. Whatever your preferred style of parenting, knowing yourself well can only be an asset.

Knowing yourself means spending ample time in solitude and really grappling with what you believe, as well as what you do not believe. Consistently set aside some time each day, at least fifteen minutes, perhaps to read about spirituality, or simply to meditate, and allow your inner feelings to emerge. As you decide what matters most to you, you'll learn a great deal about yourself and who you *really* are.

Therefore, it is crucial that you come to terms with your faith and/or doubt concerning the notion of God and other important spiritual ideas. Let's turn to your beliefs and consider them in some detail. Examining your own beliefs should make you a more informed adult, parent, and a valuable confidante for your child as he or she grows up.

What Are Your Beliefs?

In the marvelously profound book *The Meaning and End of Religion* (1963), religious writer Wilfred Cantwell Smith speaks about the place of faith in the greater order of things. Theology is part of our earthly tradition, Smith contends, while the ultimate Truth lies in the heart of God. Between the two is faith—our best guess at what the Truth may be. Faith is very accessible, Smith tells us, because it resides in the heart of man. We need to look into our hearts to find faith.

Indeed, faith is a very individual thing because it is based on individual choices. While we may share some beliefs in common, or collect these beliefs as religious dogma, our deepest aspirations and fears are peculiar to each of us as human beings. They are directly related to who we are and how we understand our purpose in life.

As a parent, knowing what you believe is the best way to offer your child a package of important ideas about religion and a sense of direction with which to proceed. But always remember that faith is not a matter of objective evidence, not a finite thing to be measured, but a subjective experience—assessed only by the strength of your convictions.

The origin of a person's belief in God is ordinarily a sense of what it is like to feel God's presence. What is it like to feel close to God? Think about what makes you confident that there is a God. Think about the warmth and love that God can provide. Get in touch with your beliefs by trying to experience the God in and around you. This kind of reflection can help you focus on such important subjects as God's relevance in your life, the role of religion in your family and your beliefs about the meaning of life, death, and afterlife. Such reflection can help you in clarifying your own image of God.

What do you believe? Like so many pivotal questions relevant to spiritual matters, it is a simple question with an endlessly complex set of answers for every person. But try to think about specific topics that concern you and seem to recur in your life, and you will begin to grab hold of this elusive question. For example, do you believe that God participates in your own life? How or how not? Is God loving, punitive, or indifferent?

Consider the practical, positive effects of believing in God. That is one of the most crucial aspects of faith that you can communicate to your child. How does believing in God contribute to your life in a positive way?

Some people feel that God provides them with a sense of strength and personal integrity. Other people stress that believing in God provides them with good feelings about themselves and about other people. Still others emphasize that God offers a central purpose for their lives, and God's commandments reveal a coherent and meaningful way to live. However you believe God contributes to your life, be clear about what God does for you.

Samantha, a forty-year-old mother of three, speaks about her own realization of God's benign role in her life. "God helps me in so many ways it is hard to describe. God has given me three beautiful children to love. But God has also shown me how to bring them up. How to have patience with them too. And God has helped me show them values to believe in. Maybe that's old-fashioned. But having a personal relationship to God has made me a better person. People tell me I'm a really good mother, but that personal relationship to God is my secret!"

While thinking about why God is important to you, you might also want to clarify why you adhere to your particular religion or theological perspective. What does your religious identification add to your life? Why are you one religion and not another?

Parents will differ concerning how religious worship enhances their lives and the lives of their families. The key thing in terms of your child is to figure out the positive messages of your religion. That way, you can offer your child a sensible explanation for your choice of religion.

To evaluate your religious preference, bear in mind such common factors as: sense of community, a setting within which to worship God, educational advantages, as well as a sense of tradition about which you feel proud. These are just a few of the benefits that parents typically attribute to religious participation and that children commonly understand. But you must determine what specific benefits you and your child can derive from your choice of religion.

When considering your faith, you can also ask yourself what you think about the quality of your life. Is life a happy experience or a good deal of confusion? Consider what you communicate to your child about what life offers. What is God's role in your life, as well as in your child's life thus far? The ways in which you answer these questions about life will reveal a great deal about you, including why you may be optimistic or pessimistic, how clearly you understand *why* you believe *what* you believe, and how you view concepts like justice, mercy, and faith, to name a few.

What do you believe about death? This is also a fundamental subject which you should talk about, either directly or indirectly, with your child. Decide whether you see death as a cruel blow by God, or as the natural ending of the life given by God. What will you tell your child about death? Perhaps your child has already attended a funeral and has many questions. You can help by being clear about your own ideas. Above all, consider what you would like your child to think about death.

Do you believe in an afterlife? What do you think it might be like? Maybe you envision a peaceful heaven, where friends and family reunite; or perhaps your ideas are less conventional. Your child already has his or her own ideas. Consider what you believe, and then you will be prepared to discuss this with your child.

Children often have elaborate pictures of hell. Do you believe in hell? What would you convey to your child about such a place? What does it have to do with God?

A Unitarian mother of two and a college professor, Ellen openly discusses her view of a hereafter. "There's no doubt in my mind that there's too much hellfire and damnation talk behind most religions. I believe in a heaven but I tell my children every person, man or woman, must find that in his own way. Hell—I don't know about that. It certainly can't be a big furnace. That's silly folklore—right out of Dante. But there might be a waiting room for some people, so to speak."

You have your own view too, even if you subscribe to the teachings of a formal religion. If you had to tell your child right now, what would you say the purpose of your life is? And, how would you respond if your child wanted to know what the purpose of his or her life might be? Prepare a direct response even if your reaction includes the admission of uncertainty. In doing so, your child will soon learn there are no facile answers to spiritual questions. Remember to ask your child to list a few possible purposes, then discuss each one. Suggest a few additional purposes and also explain that God may reveal a divine purpose to your child later on in his life.

Ultimately, your spiritual communication with your child will revolve around your respective notions of God. Therefore, your self-exploration should include the question: "How do I imagine God?"

Your image of God is important for its own merits, but it is doubly significant because your child may try to emulate it or form an opposite image. Your image of God is also a testament to your accumulated experience and learning, so it is anything but independent from your life experiences. If you take it seriously, without rigidly editing what you envision, you're bound to grow personally from this examination of faith.

There are many, many questions you can ask yourself about what you believe regarding God as a universal Being, if in fact you see God in this light. First, think about the size and scope of your version of God. Is God limitless? What role does God play in the lives of men and women, as well as children? Is this a God that is ever present from birth to death? How does God accomplish spiritual tasks? Does God merely will an event to happen, or are spiritual actions more subtle than that? These subjects will help you begin to draw your comprehensive view of God.

Consider your feelings toward God as you concentrate on your image. How fervently do you actually feel about God? Would you say that you love God? Your level of emotional involvement is important since your child will naturally pick up on this. That impression may in turn influence how significant God becomes for your youngster.

Whatever your image of God, and however pronounced your faith, it is useful to list God's perceived characteristics and your beliefs about God. Beyond using that as an introductory task, you may want to attempt to draw a portrait of God. What do you see about yourself in your depiction of God? How much of yourself have you displaced onto your vision of God? As you answer these questions, you should learn a great deal about yourself and your religious ideas.

You may wish to compare your current image of God with how you might have drawn God when you were your child's age. How has your inner portrait changed, if in fact it has? Have major life events affected that change? In what way?

Another way to arrive at similar discoveries is to pose this inquiry: "How is my view of God different from my parents' and how did it get that way?" By placing yourself in the child's role for a moment, it may help you empathize with your own daughter's or son's perspective.

"I think both my parents were absolutely convinced God was at our Mass in a priest's robe," laughed thirty-seven-year-old Bob, a Catholic father of four. "They always see God in conventional ways, connected to sacraments or to the Church. I'm not nearly so sure about God. I guess I was sort of the rebellious one in the family, compared to my brothers and sisters. I always saw God as a cowboy or as a devilish kind of character, like George Burns. [Laughs.] But I guess if I had to say now, I'm only beginning to believe in a God that you can't put in human terms."

Everyone has a story like Bob's to tell, a tale of family myths and images—you do too. Be sure not to conceal this from your current family members! Everyone, especially your child, has a great deal to learn from an exchange of religious images.

Whether this exploration of your own faith will be useful depends on how you actually convey it to your child. As the last part of your self-awareness task, summarize what you want your child to know about your faith. Try to be simple and succinct about your beliefs. Faith, like culture, is at least partly communicable. It is possible to tell your child what your heart tells you is the truth.

What About Your Doubt?

Every person I have ever met, including theologians and devout churchgoers, has occasional doubts about God. Without doubt, there can be no true faith since faith requires some element of uncertainty.

Dealing with your doubt is essential, for overcoming it enables you to maintain a positive, joyful image of God. Many people find it difficult to admit their doubts for fear of being criticized. Some other people find living with doubt more comfortable and are unable to allow a ray of hope about God's loving qualities into their lives. Where do you stand regarding doubt about God's existence or God's nature?

"Let's put it this way," clarifies forty-six-year-old Ron, a father of three and a Methodist by birth. "It's hard to make sense of why God isn't visible, isn't more obvious to us on a day-to-day basis. I feel bad because I find myself avoiding the issue, but I do wonder what it's all about."

Ron is hardly alone in reporting that he experiences episodes of doubting, although those moments can in themselves be quite lonely. John, a forty-year-old Catholic father of four, describes such an occurrence.

"When I was twenty-two, my father died of a heart attack. I can remember how I felt to this day," John recounted with hesitation. "I had just begun working at an insurance company, and the call came at work. I was not ready. I felt betrayed. I decided then and there that there was no God. I can't describe the emptiness. It took me about a year before I would go to confession again. I guess you could say that was the longest time of doubting and confusion I ever went through."

In order to address your doubts as an individual and as a parent, you should first examine what it means to doubt. You must realize that there is much ambiguity in life and countless choices to be made; doubting is a plausible response. Doubting is built into the fabric of living. Particularly when circumstances are painful and even tragic, as they were for John as a young man, doubting can be a very human and natural reaction.

As a parent, it is essential that you ask yourself, "Do I believe it is okay to doubt God or doubt the presence of God?" You must come to terms with whether skepticism is acceptable to you. Why or why not? Reflect on that question before you talk at length to your child, or before you introduce your son or daughter to the nuances of formal religious teaching.

I have found it useful to decipher where the seeds of doubt began. What sense about religious doubt did you get during childhood? Was it okay to doubt in front of your own parents? In some families, doubting is encouraged or even required. Was that true for your family?

Consider how you respond to religious doubt. Do you become curious and do you look farther into questions of faith and doubt? Or does doubt tend to make you move away and withdraw? To communicate with your child, openness, even about issues that make you feel guilty or uncomfortable, is necessary. Your child needs to feel that religious discussions will not end with a closed door.

The purpose of your self-examination concerning doubt is to help you deal with your child's doubts about God. Since children begin by thinking about what is most accessible, and they begin to think abstractly during the middle childhood years, the notion of an invisible God is difficult to have faith in. As a committed parent, you must ask yourself: "How comfortable am I with my child's doubts?"

"You have to be patient with your kids," says thirty-five-year-old Pam, an Episcopal mother of three. "You can't expect kids to believe in God just like that. [Pam snaps her fingers.] God just seems like a big myth to them at first, a big guy in the sky. How does a kid know? You have to show your kid how God appears. Still there will be doubt. You have to expect that—just like with adults."

The sense of preparedness that Pam implies is very important. The more you anticipate doubt or faith in your child, the more adept you will be at responding to your child's needs. You must be a guide who comfortably deals with whatever arises in the spiritual development of your child as his interest in faith and doubt unfolds. If doubts about God are part of your child's concerns, then you must be ready to speak and listen in a sensitive parental manner.

Dealing With Difficult Feelings: Fear, Anger, and Guilt

Self-understanding requires that a parent be willing to explore his or her darker side—the part of the personality where anxieties and conflicts reside. The great student of psychology and religion Carl Jung called this part of a person the shadow. The darker side of personality is very significant in relation to spiritual development, since it can influence how we view God. Our darker sides can distort our religious outlook in whole or in part. When it comes to ideas about God in particular, you should be aware of three commonly experienced but difficult feelings: fear, anger, and guilt.

Fear

It's helpful to begin with fear because that feeling is more accessible for most people. If tomorrow any one of us were to meet God, who among us would not be afraid? The notion of God is an awesome idea. Formal religions and popularized depictions suggest a God who is a supernatural monolith, an enormous and omnipotent Deity beyond our comprehension. Such expectations about God are bound to render even an ardent believer a bit anxious. Confronted with the presence of God, perhaps we would not be able to stand the experience—as some religions tell us.

So we bring a certain amount of fear of God into parenthood. There is a central question that a parent must ponder. "Am I afraid of the possibility of God?"

This question is something you must take seriously as an individual. While it is quite common and even natural, according to many theologians the fear of God can bluntly inhibit the development of faith. It is difficult to think intensively about something you fear, and it will be similarly difficult to entertain the same subject with your child. It is important that you examine the source of your fears before you talk with your youngster. You may fear that you have been negligent in your lack of religious involvement, or alternatively, you may feel that you retain some ill-advised beliefs. Expecting a judgmental God, you may be thinking to yourself: what if God finds out?

But of course most fears about God are really our own

irrational worries and concerns. Unknowingly, we transfer our everyday personal preoccupations onto our religious views. As a parent, it is crucial that you sort out these fears from more reasonable concerns. You can determine this best by looking at other spheres of your life. Do these fears emerge in other areas such as work or family life? Do they resemble fears you experience in relation to other authority images besides God? If so, you should talk with your spouse about them. But you should always realize that the origin of your fears may have less to do with God than with your own insecurities.

The second question, "What if there is no God?" is more troubling than the first. People who have been reared to believe steadfastly in God (and do profess belief) find probing for doubt and disbelief feels awkward or sinful. But just as you must probe your other doubts, you should stop to examine how you feel when you doubt the existence of God. Do you feel empty or liberated? If God does not exist, how would that change the way you lead your life? These are ideas that your child will grapple with at one juncture or another.

Anger

We may understand anger at God in part as a response to fear, yet anger can also be a reaction to personal trials and tribulation. Do you ever feel angry at God? For many people, life presents considerable uncertainty and all-too-frequent pain, so anger is a common response. Difficulties encountered as a parent can be a springboard for anger at God—over a child's senseless illness or death, for example.

The underlying issue is whether your image is one of

an angry God. Do you see God as vengeful, punishing, rigid, or insensitive? If so, that could be a meaningful indicator of the anger you maintain toward God. What many people do is reverse their angry feelings, so God is seen as angry, rather than the person himself. Children regularly do that too, as you may have noted with your own child. Coming to terms with any negativity in the inner portrait of God can help a person appreciate the reasons for his or her anger. For you, it can help you cope with any anger at God your youngster may express. As someone who can recognize his or her own dark, angry side when it relates to God, you should find yourself quite conversant with your child's bitterness if it arises. This is necessary if animosity and pain are to be curtailed early in a child's life.

If you discover that your image of God is an angry representation, you can try to locate the basis of that angry element. Was your image always an angry image? Have there been particular events that have been instrumental in the development of these angry characteristics? Also, have some aspects of this angry image already been transmitted to your son or daughter, perhaps along with more positive qualities?

Above all, you must not be critical of yourself or your child if there are angry elements in either person's imagery. This can be a highly volatile and divisive topic, so be careful not to overreact. Discuss your ideas with your spouse or a close friend or companion before you speak with your child. Your spouse can provide an excellent screening function, helping you filter troublesome personal material and determine how to be there for your child. Spouses also need to be noncritical and tolerant. At the same time, both parents should keep in mind that excessive religious anger can be frightening for impressionable youngsters.

When you do speak with your child, you might say something like: "Sometimes we get angry at God because we are upset or confused. Because we can't know the reasons for everything, it is understandable that we occasionally get angry. But it is best to talk it out with each other rather than keep it inside."

Guilt

Barbara, age forty-two, who grew up with one Protestant and one Catholic parent, but has raised her children in the Protestant tradition, speaks about problems of conscience. Barbara is diffident about her views and needed encouragement to speak freely. Once she was ready, she had this to say: "I don't feel it is right for religion to be a thing people are afraid is watching them, so they don't make a wrong move. It's hard to live like that. But when I was growing up, that was what I was taught. With my own children, I try to be very lenient with them. I don't want them to feel bad if they make a mistake once in a while. Nobody's perfect. I believe God understands that."

No matter what their religion or family background, many people like Barbara grow up with too much guilt surrounding religious ideas. It is especially difficult for religions which concentrate upon sin not to cultivate a degree of guilt in followers, and some of that guilt may have nothing to do with God. Some guilt is just needless suffering.

Because of miscommunication and misunderstandings in childhood, people take guilt about beliefs and practices into their adult years. In fact, most of us still retain some of the same guilty feelings we had as children even as we prepare to become parents ourselves. But what is this guilt about?

Sometimes religious guilt is the result of our own anger or doubt, such as the flashes of guilt people may feel when they invoke God's name in a curse. At other times, people experience guilt about something very different—like the sexual or aggressive drives. If these drives become associated with religious belief, the result for the individual can be very confusing. It is hard to know how to determine the source of any guilt, especially guilt that is grounded in religious issues.

It is crucial that you try to understand why guilt exists and work through it as best you can. Otherwise, through child-rearing and the home environment, you may unconsciously pass along unnecessary guilt to your child. Beware of issuing too many directives to your child, such as: "You should pray everyday!" Try to avoid guilt-inducing comments: "You don't have to go to church, even though it would make me feel better!" In all cases concerning religion, the best way to avoid guilt is to think of your comments' effects on your child. Anticipate how your comment will be received, what your child may or may not do as a result, and—most importantly—whether your child will most likely be responding authentically, or from guilt.

A parent needs to figure out whether he or she experiences guilt toward God and how that guilt may be manifested. You must try to recognize guilt that is unnecessary (e.g., guilt about sexuality). Then you can turn to your relationship with your child and consider the element of guilt there.

The difficult feeling of guilt, along with the unrelenting experiences of fear and anger concerning religion, create anguish for many people. The key thing to remember is not to avoid them, as uncomfortable as they can be. Consider talking to another adult with whom you feel comfortable about these personal feelings. The most helpful and commonly applied ways to deal with religious guilt, fear, or anger are: telling worries to a spouse, confiding in a friend or coworker, speaking to a sibling or parent, and disclosing to a clergyperson or psychotherapist. Find a way that feels best for you, then concentrate on your own religious views and your role as a parent.

By experiencing faith and confronting doubt and difficult feelings, you have the opportunity to reach deeper into your soul and place your inner life in greater psychological order. By facing your guilt, fear, and anger, you will make the task of communicating with your child much lighter. As you grow more self-aware, you will be free to fully attend to the spiritual needs of your son or daughter.

PART TWO

INTRODUCING
YOUR
CHILD TO GOD

Talking to Your Child: Getting Started

"Dear God,
  I love you more than any body else that I do not know.

                    Walt
                    (age 10)"
                    FROM PRIVATE COLLECTION

Many couples are eager to discuss God and religious issues with their children but are uncertain about when to begin. It is best to begin when your child is about four or five years old—but only if your child is showing signs of curiosity and interest. It is essential not to push a youngster into something he or she is not ready for. That is how many children develop negative feelings about religion.

By being attentive to your child's questions and curiosity, you will be able to detect a readiness to talk about religion. While children tend to differ dramatically in maturity, most youngsters ask about natural phenomena and life events well before the age of five. For example, they may ask about daytime and nighttime, or about being asleep and being awake.

Also, children may be contemplative at important family times, such as a religious holiday, when a younger sibling is born, or when a beloved grandparent dies. When you notice that your child is particularly moved and open to discovery, it is an excellent time to begin talking about religion.

But what is the best thing to say? You do not have to be an expert on religion to talk about God with your child. All you need is to be yourself, willing to share your own thoughts and pragmatic wisdom. It is best to begin with the practical, accessible events of family life and your child's world, such as family meals, school activities, mom's and dad's occupations, neighbors, relatives, and entertaining hobbies and happenings. Begin by speaking about familiar subjects, and then discuss how each is related to God or to religion. For example, you might say that God is involved in your relationship to other people because God teaches us to love our neighbors. That simple approach is the easiest and most effective means of religious communication. Some parents look only to others for religious wisdom, or sadly, shy away from conversations with their child for fear of not knowing enough. They might push away their child by saying, "Ask your Sunday School teacher." You are a much deeper store of religious experience than you realize and of infinitely more value to your child's learning than anyone else.

Whether you are trying to teach your child a specific point or merely discussing the notion of God in general with your child, please *always* keep in mind one quintessential idea:

FOCUS ON GOD'S PRESENCE IN THE EVERYDAY LIFE OF YOUR CHILD

Too esoteric or remote a discussion will not be meaningful for your child. Too vague a discussion will disappoint you as well, for I suspect that your primary interests are to grow closer to your son or daughter and to help your child to grow. Moreover, an exclusively intellectual or rote discussion will seem boring and tedious to both of you, and you will soon lose interest in any spiritual explorations.

When the time feels appropriate, begin by concentrating on a specific event and see where that leads your child and you. For example, if a newborn has just arrived, you will probably notice curiosity and change in your other children. You may choose to discuss God's role in the birth with the baby's five-year-old brother. You can begin by asking him how he feels about the birth and why he thinks it came about. Once he has the opportunity to express himself, you may choose to offer a religious explanation for the birth. For instance, the new baby may be viewed as God's gift to your family. Then apply this to his birth too. Often, a young child is threatened by the arrival of a baby sister or brother. Consider the comments of six-year-old Albert, upon hearing the news that he now has a little brother—born on December 24. "It's *still* my Christmas," Albert asserted, "but he can stay and watch." How is God involved in your child's happiness and well-being—despite his new competition? There is no better way to cultivate your child's interest than to make God personally meaningful to him at the outset.

Once his or her curiosity is evident, another way to start discussion is simply to ask your child, "Have you heard of God?" "What is God like?" "What do you think about God?" and "Who is God?" You will need to be patient, but don't be surprised if your child has quite a bit to say. Even young children pick up a great deal of information and ideas from television and their siblings, as well as from adult conversations. Of course your child may also express confusion or a lack of knowledge, but that is the opportunity for you to begin talking about what you personally believe.

The most conventional and the most direct way is by deciding to introduce the notion of God to your child and beginning to teach about your beliefs. You can start by saying, "I want to tell you about a person called God." Then you can proceed to describe how you imagine God. The advantages of this approach are its clarity and directness. Older children are familiar with this method of learning, since it is similar to the way they learn at school. However, the drawback to this method is that it doesn't explicitly invite your child to express himself or herself or to explore religious questions that emerge. So it is important that you both explain your beliefs fully and also ask about your child's beliefs. Otherwise, your child will learn about institutional depictions of God and about your ideas of God, but may not develop his own individual notion.

Begin With Your Own Beliefs

While keeping in mind your child's age and gender, you must begin by sharing your beliefs with your child.

You have the right if not the moral obligation to let

your child know what you believe about God. But more importantly, your dialogue will be mutual and heartfelt if you express your own views. Your beliefs will matter a great deal to your child, though they should not be the child's only source of information.

Your lack of free expression would deprive your child in many ways. How else can your child learn about his or her rich religious heritage? What better way for your child to get to know you better as a person?

Eight-year-old Mark, a Lutheran youngster, comments: "I talk with my dad every night about God. My dad thinks God is like a man; big and strong. I think God is more like a spirit. Maybe we're both partly right. Anyway, I like it when we talk about big ideas."

Elaine, a thirty-seven-year-old Catholic mother of three, has this to say about describing her faith: "I never thought I would be so religious. But when I had kids, I realized the importance of giving them something to believe in. I tell my kids about all the years I stopped going to church, too. I tell them why. And I tell them why I started going again."

Children like Mark, and parents like Elaine, know the importance of making religious views explicit. When you engage your child, get started in the right way. Tell your child what you believe and why; talk about how God fits into your life. Tell about how God helped you overcome feeling unpopular or being afraid of the dark when you were a child. And tell him who or what you think God is. If you do all of that, you will pique your child's interest and curiosity.

Some parents do not want to express their own beliefs to their children. Often, their own parents were dogmatic and domineering, and they do not want to repeat such a pattern. Afraid to impose religious imagery on their children, they also miss out on exchanging ideas with their youngsters, and their parent-child relationship suffers as a consequence.

Other parents inundate their youngsters with religious ideas and don't allow their children to think and speak for themselves. They feel they must protect their child from incorrect or immoral ideas by teaching a set way of living. Don't be overly shy or unduly dogmatic with your child. Try to strike a balance between revealing your own beliefs and eliciting your child's ideas. If you can accomplish that, your child will learn to appreciate and respect your views as well as his or her own.

Begin by Encouraging Your Child

Opening up is one of two basic things a parent needs to do in order to communicate spiritually with a child. The other thing is encouraging your child to speak. That isn't always a simple matter, particularly with children who are naturally reticent. But it is vital. How else can your child tell you how he or she feels?

Your child may require a gentle push to open up and express his thoughts about God and the world. Many children do. After all, ideas about God are very complicated and not easy to talk about. God is an ambiguous and intimidating notion for most adults, so we cannot always expect children to enter into discussion. Then again, sometimes children can surprise us with their facility for talking about God.

"I love to talk about God," acknowledges twelve-year-old Artie. "I like to show how much I know and I like to find out more. It is all so interesting, how God has a purpose for everything."

Artie comes from a religious family, so the subject of God is very familiar to him. But even children from less observant families often have clear and compelling ideas about God. You may have fewer expectations of your own child, but be prepared for the possibility that your child may have many distinct ideas about God.

Remember to tell your child why you think it is important to talk about God. Tell your child openly that you love him very much and you want to get to know his thoughts. Tell your child why God is an important part of your life or why not. Discuss God's importance in family tradition, one that involves grandparents and aunts and uncles too. Talk about how God is celebrated at your place of worship, if you have one, and tell your child why it is important to worship God.

But don't just tell your child things. *Ask* your child too. For example, is he or she curious about how the world began? Here is a nine-year-old's account of how God wrote the Bible: "God could have got somebody else to do it like all the modern people do but He wanted to do it Himself. It took Him a very long time. Almost two months. He got a little tired of it. He found someone to check His spelling and He saw that it was good. He added the parts about Jesus later. Then it was all around so everybody could read it and learn. God was very pleased, so He decided to rest. He is glad that the book is still popular today." Asking is one of the nicest ways to say to your child: "I love you and respect you as an individual."

You can best encourage your child to explore religious ideas by making any talk or activity fun and enjoyable. *Religious* does not necessarily mean solemn and ascetic; it can suggest liveliness and joy too; it's very important to keep that in mind. Put yourself in your child's position. What does he or she enjoy? Encourage your child by presenting God in the context of what your child loves. For example, if your child enjoys sports you might ask what God has to do with baseball or soccer. Perhaps you can point out that God gave us healthy, strong bodies. If your child loves music, you might ask if his or her favorite song has any connection with God. God gave us ears to appreciate sound, voices to sing, etc. Remember, you are the one who must introduce your child and God to each other. By talking about God in the context of your child's world, the idea of God will become more and more natural.

How Do Children Differ?

If you have more than one child, or if you want to better appreciate the origins of children's images of God, it is important to be aware of the ways that children differ. No two God images are exactly alike, and membership in the same family does not ensure similar religious ideas. Children tend to differ significantly, depending on their age, gender, personality, temperament, and family dynamics.

Your child's age is most important because a child's capacity for thinking grows with time.

Ages Four–Six

Children from ages four to six can make some basic connections between a Creator and life events. They can discuss how the world was made and how God may influence the world right now. They also understand that people can have different points of view about religion. They can remember the names of different religious groups, like Baptists and Lutherans, and often understand these distinctions like they do other familiar distinctions, such as Red Sox and Yankees. Sometimes, unless told otherwise, they may picture religious groups competing against each other. Four- to six-year-olds are inclined to see life in positive terms; they range from reasonable optimism to Pollyannaish thinking. Many will describe a simple, fun-loving God, but few will become heavily involved in explaining global problems in terms of religion. They may refer to "world hunger" or "wars that people have," but their solutions are inclined to be facile, and God's role is not seen as significant. Because their thinking is mostly literal, they are highly responsive to historical accounts and their parents' opinions about history—both biblical and personal. While their opinions about religion sometimes seem rote and socialized, they are capable of spontaneity and surprising wisdom.

A five-year-old Jewish youngster, Howard, provides a religious commentary which typifies members of his age group. "There's a Jewish God and there's a Christian God," Howard explains. "Both are good Gods. They create different activities for the people—like sports. But if you're Jewish, it doesn't hurt to do a Christian sport, and if you're Christian, it doesn't hurt to do a Jewish sport."

From Howard's description, it's not clear which religious group is responsible for old-time sports like walking on water, but it is evident that Howard is trying to make sense of religious distinctions. He allows that people can have different points of view, or even separate Gods. Howard is quite open-minded in his opinions and grants each of the religions equal status on his spiritual turf.

Parents of four- to six-year-olds like Howard may wish to rely heavily on drawings of God as the focus of religious exchange. Asking children to draw pictures and fantasize playing God allows them to express themselves in a fun and nonthreatening manner. With regard to play, have your child choose a favorite doll or toy and ask him to show what God might say or do with these personal items. You can ask your child, "Does God like this little doll?" or "What does God wish to say to the little doll?" It's best to keep any discussions straightforward and reasonably simple. If you get too complex, your child may become confused and give up. For these smallest youngsters, action-oriented strategies are the most informative and useful. Say to your child, "Why don't you move the dolls around?" Most four- to six-year-olds can express themselves best through activity and role-playing, rather than through verbalization alone.

Because of their enduring quality, drawings in particular can be a continual source of conversation even as your child gets older. You might consider having your child do an annual drawing of God, so that you can keep a record of how his or her ideas about God change.

Ages Seven–Nine

Children between the ages of seven and nine are more abstract in their thinking about God. Unlike younger children, these boys and girls don't take everything their parents say so literally. This means that if your child is between those ages, he or she can consider hypothetical situations and more intangible things like brotherhood and miracles. Your child may wonder where dreams come from, or whether God is with a person when he or she is alone. Unlike the five- or six-year-old, your older youngster may readily think about what is not visible and evident.

At this age, your child may evidence both wishes and fears about God, and you should notice less certainty in your child's beliefs. Children of this age group frequently accept institutional or formal religious explanations of God's nature, yet harbor underlying questions, doubts, and fears. They are very aware of ideas about God that are taught by church or school figures, or those notions portrayed by television and the media. Thus, you may find your child affected by a minister's sermon or attentive to an episode of the TV show *Highway to Heaven.* You may also observe, however, a certain readiness for more exploration which lies just below the surface of your child's comments.

Storytelling directly from the Bible and making up stories are excellent ways for parents to communicate with seven- to nine-year-old children. They readily identify with characters and are becoming interested in the connection of people's lives. They like drama and stories mixed with formal learning and imagination, providing a colorful picture of God and religion. One eight-year-old that I know is particularly fond of the biblical story of Jacob. Time and time again, he asks his mother to tell him the story or read about it from a children's book. Whether it's fighting with the angel or receiving Isaac's blessing, Jacob is a figure that my eight-year-old friend quickly identifies with. The youngster seems attracted to the character of Jacob because Jacob is his own middle name, and because he sees the biblical character as tough and brave. Perhaps your child has his or her own favorite character—find out who it is.

Ages Ten–Twelve

Children between the ages of ten and twelve make more inquiries about God and about the world than their younger siblings. They are much more verbal and sophisticated, and are apt to assert expertise on any number of subjects. Some are less fearful about expressing religious doubts since by now they have learned that doubting is natural. Others lack confidence concerning their opinions but are still filled with knowledge learned from school or outside experiences. Try to tap their knowledge as much as possible, for demonstrating what he or she knows will make religious conversations more pleasurable for your child.

These older children have already experienced some frustrations and disappointments in their young lives. Such experiences as being hurt playing in a sport or not being chosen for a role in a school play are often tied to religious doubt and skepticism, for they tend to make children wonder why God isn't more helpful. They will enable you to determine the meaning your child attaches to negative experiences. Try to get to know your child better spiritually through setbacks as well as through triumphs. Ask your child, "Is something bothering you?" or "Can I help?"

Older children may still describe God in human terms and picture God in human forms, but God's image may well coexist with more spiritlike depictions. God may be presented as "divine" or "floating like a cloud." See if you can detect this quality in your child's imagery and encourage your child to explore further. Is God more like a spirit or more like a person, or is God something entirely different? That can give you a good idea of how tangible God is for your child.

Nine- to twelve-year-old children may indicate a particular fascination with the idea of afterlife. These elements in your child's ideas about God will also help reveal worries and concerns.

Twelve-year-old Lorraine offers a remarkably tranquil view of the future, allowing only a bit of anxiety at the conclusion of her comments. "God is a Being like no other Being. God is invisible and is beyond our understanding. Even a minister's. But God is involved with people in a different way. God helps people to make a change to a different place after they die. I think Heaven is real peaceful. I think life is a search for peace." Because of a close and candid relationship with her mother, Lorraine has been able to develop a sensible theological perspective.

Parents can comfortably initiate frank question-and-answer discussions with children of this age group. Having children write letters to God can also prove colorful and informative as well. But here are a few sample questions you may want to consider when speaking about God with your oldest children.

1. How old is God?
2. Is it possible to communicate with God? How?
3. What would you like to change about God?
4. What does God have to do with the positive things that happen to you?
5. What does God have to do with pain or injuries?

Suggestions for Getting Started

In the beginning, you will be able to reach your child best by concentrating on those concerns that really matter to your child, such as parent-child relations, sibling feelings, and friendship. Since you've been with your child throughout his or her young life, you possess a great appreciation for your child's experiences, temperament, and way of seeing things. If you use this information when you approach your child, you will probably find him or her more receptive. Instinctively, children have a desire to get closer to God. You can count on that, too.

Below are general suggestions that many people find helpful in initiating this conversation. They may help to stimulate your own preparation or provide a list of possibilities to consider. Be sure to use these suggestions according to your child's readiness and curiosity.

Twenty Suggestions for Getting Started

1. Ask your child to write a letter to God. Letters are a wonderful way for a child to express things he or she might not say directly. Letters to God can be a form of prayer, a means of confession or even a shopping list! So be prepared. Here is a favorite example:

   "Dear God, Who do you pray to? If you don't say prayers, do you think you can let me off the hook?

   Jim
   (age nine)"
   FROM *DEAR GOD*

2. Ask your child what he or she thinks about your church or synagogue services.

3. Take your child out for an ice cream cone. Ask your child how he or she thinks ice cream and other good things came to be. It's a fine way to initiate discussion about the origin of the universe. Selecting a familiar object like an ice cream cone or flowers or pets can make your talk more accessible for your child.

4. If one of your child's grandparents is deceased, ask your child where he thinks grandma or grandpa is. Be ready to offer a thoughtful explanation.

5. Take your child out on a clear summer night and take a look at the stars. Ask your child what is out there.

6. Take a long walk in the snow, in some nearby woods, or along a quiet beach, and ask your child if he or she has wondered who "invented" trees, sand, snow, etc.

7. Play art class with your child. Suggest that you each try to make your own drawings of God. Be sure to do the drawings in color, so that your child can express a full range of feelings about his or her notions.

8. Read to your child from a children's book of Bible stories and ask your child what he or she thought about the story. Did your child believe it really happened?

9. When your child asks you about some significant family event (e.g., your nephew's bar mitzvah, your cousin's wedding), try to explain the ceremony and rituals in terms of God.

10. On the eve of a major religious holiday (e.g., Christmas, Rosh Hashanah), try to explain to your child how God is really the quiet force which inspires that holiday.

11. If your child has experienced a big disappointment recently, such as losing an important basketball game or having a trip canceled, find out why he or she thinks it

happened. Does your child blame God for disappointments?

12. Read aloud a poem about religion or spirituality and
discuss its meaning. Ask your child what comes to
mind when he or she hears the poem. Choose a poem
that you are particularly fond of.

13. See a television movie (e.g., *Miracle on 34th Street*), or
go to a play with a religious theme, and ask your child
to accompany you. Find out what he or she thinks
about it. Ask your child what God has to do with it.

14. Read your child a favorite passage from the Bible and
ask your child what he or she thought it meant.

15. Tell your child that you want to have a family discussion about an important matter. Then sit down with
your child (or children) and your spouse and explain
what your beliefs and doubts about God are. Have
everyone in turn talk about their ideas. Suggest that
you have a family discussion once a week.

16. In a similar family discussion format, try a bit more
structure with your child or children. On 3″ × 5″ index
cards, print some key words for discussion and place
the cards in a pile. Have each member of your family
blindly choose a topic to talk about. Some key words
might be: PEOPLE; GOD; PEACE; CHURCH; RE-
LIGION; GOODNESS; DOUBT.

17. While you're giving your child a bath, try to see who
can name more scenes involving water in the Bible.

18. Ask your child to role-play God with a set of family
dolls. For example, ask your child: "What does God
have to say to the little boy (girl)?"

19. Along with your child, draw a simple picture of God.

20. Simply ask your child: "What's the biggest, most important thing in the whole world or universe?"

❧ 5

Discussing the Notion of God

"Dear Lady God,

I love you. And I want to thank you for making the color pink. Pink is a beautiful creation.

I think in Heaven you must have made everything pink. Pink cushions, pink houses, even pink clouds.

I just hope the boys don't feel too out of place. That would be too bad.

I love you lots,
Liz Marie
(age 7)"
FROM PRIVATE COLLECTION

"What is God like?" your child wonders and then tries to conjure an image for himself or herself. This is very important for your child, for in large part it will determine how your child develops spiritually.

Talking with a son or daughter about their notions of God is the cornerstone of spiritual communication. A child's idea of God depicts, to a great degree, a union of your child's deepest aspirations and concerns. The God image includes all kinds of fantasy images, notions of fictitious heroes, movie stars, and rock and roll stars, as well as well-known religious figures, like Moses and David and Jesus. Your task as a parent is to help your child organize and understand these images. Whatever its religious meaning, your child's image of God bears undeniable psychological significance. It's an indicator of your child's religious learning, his interpretation of family life, and a clue to his self-image.

Where Do Those Ideas About God Come From?

I am sure that you have had the common experience of discovering a number of items that your child has collected. Rocks, ribbons, pennies, parts of toys, shoelaces, even something valuable like a ring. You are amazed at their variety and number, a veritable museum. Where did he (or she) find all these things? And why these particular items? you wonder.

Children's perceptions of God are a lot like your child's treasure chest of special paraphernalia. As a parent, sometimes it will be difficult for you to know where it all came from; you have to ask in order to find out, and even then, you may not be certain. Yet there's always a fascinating story behind your child's discoveries, material or spiritual, and it pays to explore them.

So find out where your child's ideas about God came from. Start with the influence of organized religion and formal worship. Usually, such institutionalized imagery is quite visible in your child's notions, particularly if your family is significantly involved in church or religious activities.

If your family attends religious services regularly, there is probably a priest, minister, or rabbi who gives a sermon or tells a story about God. While children are famous for tuning out these talks, you may be surprised to learn how influential the clergy really are. When that religious man or woman is talking about God's power or God's great forgiveness, your child is forming his or her own mental image of what God must be like. Your child is off and running with daydreams and fantasies, especially if the youngster is attending to the speaker only part of the time. Some of that fantasizing will probably include God—because your child is busy at work in reaching a compromise between the clergyperson's imagery and his or her own.

"My rabbi talks a lot about how God saved the Jews . . . I know all about that," declares ten-year-old Brad. "The way I figure it, God must do that so we owe Him a favor!"

Children pick up ideas about God from Bible and religious stories too. Have you ever read a Bible story, parable or proverb to your child? For example, you might read the story of Exodus in order to show how God helps people through their suffering. Or you might read the story of King David to show how God can help a person fight against insurmountable odds. Most likely, your child will listen to the story and select two or three central ideas from it and create imaginative scenes in his mind. In these scenarios, God may be a shadowy figure behind the scenes or may pop up for a cameo appearance. Sometimes your child may even focus on God and elaborately imagine God's activities. The story is the inspiration, but your child will place his or her own stamp on the biblical events.

I am reminded of one seven-year-old I know, Frank, who was particularly taken with the story of Joseph in the

Old Testament. Frank liked the idea of a brightly colored coat and colorful dreams too. I am not certain that Frank digested the entire story of Joseph, his brothers, and Pharaoh, but Frank knew about the famous coat and Joseph's prophetic dream. These images stood out for him. In fact, Frank's image of God was affected by them. According to Frank, "God is a regular man with a red and black coat. God can predict the future too. He does it through dreams."

If you read a Bible passage to your child, or if your child has read a story outside the home, take the time to ask about it. Ask your child what he remembers about the passage. Ask him or her to describe God's role. What was God trying to do in the story? Finally, it can also be helpful to ask whether the story reminded your child of anything else, such as a prior experience, or "Has anything like this story ever happened in our family?"

If the Bible is not read frequently in your family, or if you do not believe in it, your child's understanding of God will be somewhat different. Some Bible stories have become so much a part of our culture that even children from nonobservant homes are aware of them. Because we refer to God all the time in the media, in the workplace, and at home, it is small wonder that children collect a vast assortment of notions about God at a young age. Some children, a vocal but decided minority, are absolutely certain they know everything there is to know about God—even the most specific details. According to eight-year-old Carl, "God lives at 11 God Street at the North Pole. He lives in a big gray mansion and has two thousand servants. But he is really good to them. He even gives them Tuesdays off so that they can visit their relatives on Earth. God pays them three hundred dollars and takes care of them. He is a good guy to work for."

Remember that your child hears about God in all kinds of ways. Every day at school, as the Pledge of Allegiance is recited, your child and all the other children invoke God's name as they salute the American flag. What could your child be thinking about at that moment? Sometime between greeting classmates and eating a peanut butter and jelly sandwich, your child is imagining something about God—every day.

Perhaps even more than school, television and the movies encourage ideas about divine forces. If your child watches only an average amount of television—about three hours a day—he or she will eventually come across a movie about Jesus or a television show that talks about God.

But television and movies may have an even greater impact in nonexplicit references to religion and spirituality. Many heroic and superheroic characters must encounter spiritual forces—both good and evil. With shows like *The Real Ghostbusters* or *Space Rangers*, the entertainment media provide an infinite number of fantasy images for children to choose from.

But how is your child processing these images? That is a vitally important question. Just as you must be concerned with what your child watches in general, you should pay particular attention to material that has spiritually related potential. Is the image of God in that movie good for your child? Be protective without being repressive. Fantasy imagery in the media can have a dramatic effect on your child, particularly if it isn't buffered by other ideas. It may provide your child with a distorted view by suggesting that God is only concerned with power and control. Alternatively, a sensitive program can open up your child's imagination by illustrating the many subtle and varied forms that God may assume.

Ultimately, the primary and most influential way that children hear about God is through their parents. You represent the most crucial source of information for your child when it comes to religion. Eventually your child will decide for himself or herself about God—but in the meantime, you are a vital wellspring of inspiration and information.

What does your child picture if you say something simple, such as "God is everywhere"? Does your child wonder if God is the grass and the concrete and the telephone lines? Does your youngster think that God is in the air, like the wind? Or does he imagine a huge monolith who roams the earth in search of action? When it comes to children's images of God, *anything* is possible. The word *infinite* must have originated to fit the endless variety of children's ideas. But it's up to you to ask and find out what your child pictures in his or her mind.

Helen, age twenty-six and religiously unaffiliated, has a five-year-old daughter, Sandy. Helen likes to play "picture games" with Sandy. That's how Helen encourages her daughter in discussing what she imagines. "I've told Sandy that the world got started a long time ago when a lot of things in space started crashing into each other. Then I ask her what she imagines. She thought for a while and said, 'Big angel moving blocks around and the blocks went Bang!' Sandy seems to think a lot about what I say, even if she's alone."

You don't need to play picture games with your child but you should be aware of the impact you have. Your child looks to you to be a model for how to think about God and how to act toward God. Even when you utter an automatic "Thank God" or "God forbid," your child is likely to be deciphering what that says about God.

What Are the Most Common Impressions That Children Have?

Given the amount of time you spend with your child, and the considerable impact that you can have, it is not surprising that family life greatly shapes the way he or she will envision God. So it's understandable why father and mother images routinely pop up when children discuss God. But your child is born with a unique temperament too, and that disposition is nurtured in your family until that child's adult personality is formed. You may find it helpful to keep assessing your child's personality from early on, so you can understand how you may have shaped his or her overall impressions of God.

Many youngsters imagine God as a big father figure, owing to the considerable paternal influence in our culture. In fact, the father figure is the most frequently occurring family influence.

When portrayed as a father, God seems to occupy the head of the human household. God provides conventionally paternal functions like protectiveness and strength. God is commonly pictured as tall or big, and is known to carry an executive sense of authority. Whether a child is a boy or a girl, God the Father occupies an elevated position and must come down to Earth to meet with His children.

"God is kind of like my father," ten-year-old Jeff states

matter-of-factly. "God has a lot of control over things, including people. He tries to tell them what to do for their own good, but they don't always listen. The people of the world should listen to God more, for He has been around much longer than they have."

If you notice that your child seems to think of God as a father, ask your child directly if they see God that way. Ask where he or she acquired ideas about God. Find out if your child thinks God is good, bad, or mixed. See if this has anything to do with you or your spouse, and try to talk through any subjects which seem significant for your child.

The second most prominent image among children is a maternal image, which is underemphasized by many people who work with children. The maternal God is a nurturing Deity, sensitive to the needs of people here on earth, especially children. This feminine God listens to people's prayers and provides a comforting, loving response. Frequently, maternal imagery in a God figure accompanies such qualities as empathy, forgivingness, and healing. A maternal God takes care of the world.

"I know that God is good and loving," nine-year-old Kari Ann reveals. "I believe that God gives us all the things we need. That's why there's cereal for breakfast and vegetables and fish for dinner. God makes sure that we stay warm and that we don't get sick. God loves us for who we are."

If you recognize maternal imagery in your child's religious ideas, ask your child about them and see if their sense of God is related to motherhood, birth, or caretaking. With boys, who may be diffident about their mother feelings, you may need to proceed a bit more cautiously. If your son is stressing a God who sounds like a father, you might ask,

"What else could God be like?" This can be an excellent way to open up other topics which he may be keeping to himself.

Not all of children's imagery is paternal or maternal. It is also represented as "God as a couple" or "God, the grandparent." Because children often think of their parents as a unit—an adult hierarchy that they are answerable to—God can appear as a two-membered board of authority. In families where there is significant and frequent contact with grandparents, these encounters are apt to influence a child's formation of religious imagery.

How can you distinguish between parent imagery and grandparent imagery? Sometimes children talk about someone older or bigger than their mom and dad. They may picture God as living a semiretired existence in heaven. Also, they may not see God as heavily involved in the daily rewards and punishment of people—the discipline of everyday life. Of course some children, like eleven-year-old Becky Sue, talk about grandparents openly when discussing their religious beliefs.

"God is a little like my grandfather. . . . He smiles a lot and fixes toys for you when you need him to," notes Becky Sue.

You can ask your own child, "Is God like any people that you know?" If you sense some influence of grandparents, you can also probe a little more directly: "What does God have to do with Grandma and Grandpa?" Be sure not to force the issue since it will only be relevant for some children. Use your good judgment as to how influential your child's grandparents are likely to be.

When you think about how you influence your child's notions of God, consider your child's own unique personality as well. What is your child's natural temperament and growing personality like? How might this affect his or her view of God? You will want to tailor your discussions about religion to the specific needs and style of your child.

One topic of great interest is the different personalities that children assign to God. Here is a summary of the different God types; your understanding of them may help you better communicate with your child about religion.

As you speak with your child, you may discover that he or she reveals a combination of these themes rather than just one God type. Remember that each type places an artificial limit on God, so that the main idea is to help your child grow in flexibility and expand his or her picture of God. Your child will also say things that don't fit into the categories that follow. That is to be expected, for children are much too individualized and unique to be captured by any simple categorization. Of course, so is God.

Along with parental images, the seven other personalities of God that I have most frequently observed among children are presented below. With each God type, I am including some questions you may want to ask if your child describes a God image that resembles it.

GOD, THE FRIENDLY GHOST

God is a congenial spirit that befriends a child and engages in play. God is lighthearted and enjoyable, even humorous at times. God greets children on casual, nonthreatening terms and sees the world pretty much as they do.

Ask your child, "What kinds of things does God like to do?" "What matters most to God?" "Is God always friendly?"

GOD, THE DISTANT THING IN THE SKY

God is experienced as real but very far away, usually "off in the clouds." God is not associated with much feeling or interest by the child, who is uncertain or confused about God. God is independent from the everyday concerns of people.

Ask your child: "Who is God?" "Is God ever close to us?" "What does God look like?" "How could things be improved by God?"

GOD, THE LOVER IN HEAVEN

A romanticized version of God in which a child imagines a human-like being full of strength or beauty. God appears as a kind of mate or spouse, and is depicted as the heroine or hero of a great myth or fairy tale. God may be the focus of much attention and yearning, since God is purported to be especially loving to children.

Ask your child: "Does everyone have the same God?" "How is it possible to communicate with God?" "Has God ever given you anything?" "What is God's home like?"

THE INCONSISTENT GOD

God is seen as being unpredictable and difficult to make sense of. A child may well express mixed feelings about God, who is there only some of the time when you need help. God is essentially twofold: a helper and a hinderer. It is hard to know which hat God will wear at any given moment.

Ask your child: "Is God good?" "Where can you find God?" "Do you have any other feelings about God?" "Was there a time that you felt let down by God?"

GOD, THE ONCE AND FUTURE KING

God seems to be the head of the government of the universe. God has tremendous power and makes laws for people to follow. God is often pictured as physically big and impressive. The people of the world, including children, live in God's territory and dominion.

Ask your child: "What kinds of powers does God have?" "Does God have a family?" "What does God want from human beings?" "How does God become so powerful?" "Is there anything that God can't do?"

GOD, THE ANGRY VILLAIN

God is considered to be mean and vindictive. God is believed to be selfish and insensitive to the needs of people. Because this Deity has an insatiable need for dominance, people are expected to give in to God's every whim. God can even be cruel and arbitrary, especially in relation to children and other innocent people.

Ask your child: "Why do you think God is mean?" "How has God been mean to you?" "Did you ever do anything that you think made God angry?"

GOD, THE THERAPIST (DR. GOD)

God emerges as a benign, helping figure who corrects all the wrongs of the world, or more typically, the child's problems. God is sensitive and empathic, and provides hope and comfort. God heals a child's [physical and emotional] injuries, and protects him from future worries. Children speak to God about their concerns, and God hears their requests.

Ask your child: "Does God know if you have a problem?" "Does God make things better?" "Does God help everyone—without exception?" "Why do some problems continue?"

Whichever of these or other God types your child seems to stress, you may notice that these personalities overlap with religious rituals and folklore learned in the home or at school. For example, as The Once and Future King, God may choose twelve disciples or summon a plague upon another kingdom. As The Angry Villain, God may command a great flood or hurl people into the sea. In this way, your child is trying to bring together the God of his or her experiences with the God suggested by formal religious teaching.

But don't expect that your child's notion of God will be fixed. The God conception should change as your child grows. After all, as children mature they are better equipped to deal with more complex theological questions and in a better position to understand themselves. As you speak with your child, look for those characteristics or clusters about God that seem to endure despite momentary changes. Is God always a benevolent ruler? Is God always temperamental? Is God always powerful? Answering these questions will help you see the imagery that forms the bases of your child's ideas.

Do you notice any similarities or differences between your child's notion of God and your own? Then address them. You may wish to introduce the thought that two people can have very different ideas and still love each other a lot. That will help your child understand his or her own separateness as a person, and perhaps get to appreciate you better too.

What Sex Is God?

Along with age, your child's gender is likely to affect his or her view of God. Gender is important because boys and girls are socialized to think and act differently about a host of topics, and religion is one of them. While sex roles have been changing dramatically over the last fifteen years, gender-related ideas about religion have been around for centuries and are not likely to change quickly. While references to God as "She" are emerging among some religious groups and individuals, and these departures from convention may help expand our thinking about God, most children are still socialized to believe that God is a "He." Keep abreast of your child's view of God's gender, and remain alert to the masculine and feminine qualities that their God image displays.

Boys have a tendency to see God in rational and physical terms. In their descriptions of the Deity, they are quick to emphasize intelligence, size, and strength. "It's a great big God who has all the knowledge in the world," sums up one eight-year-old. God is depicted as the definitive master of the universe and his dominion is unlimited. For boys, power is a central trait, and they will speak about it at great length when you ask them about God. You may wish to ask your son, "How powerful do you think God is?" Then talk to your son about the possible uses and limits of power in his life. For example, you might say that people have the power to stop wars and make peace in the world but have had difficulty in accomplishing that goal. You might add that it is up to future generations like his to keep striving for peace.

Boys are inclined to visualize God as "manlike" and tend to identify with this great masculine figure. They are more likely than girls to openly announce that they wish to "be like God," as if God were a divine role model or a superhero. Boys also speak candidly about God's role in people's lives. They often relate God to well-known events like World War II or to scientific concepts like gravity or the solar system. The boys that I have interviewed have had a great deal to say when you ask them, "How did God create the world?" They have been outspoken when you ask them, "What does God have to do with war?" One nine-year-old offered this somber response to me: "God is like a book writer who is writing the book of history. All the wars are part of the action. (Pause.) I wonder why it has to be that way?"

But what happens when you ask a male youngster about the possibility of a female God? Boys are basically uncomfortable with the idea. They become anxious and sometimes try to push away the notion. It is as if a female figure in a powerful position is frightening and intimidating. "If God were female," ten-year-old Dan nervously explained, "things would be a mess. The guys would be in a lot of trouble. God would treat us as second-class citizens. Maybe God would not have made us be born!" In any case, you may find it interesting to carefully ask your son if God could be female.

Girls, on the other hand, are more placid and reflective on the whole. They describe God as aesthetic and spiritlike, while God does seem to retain a surface masculinity. Nonetheless, God is frequently associated with creativity, art, and music. God's lyrical quality was captured by one seven-year-old when she surmised, "I think of God when I hear

Amy Grant songs." Girls describe a more angelic God whose love flows freely. Unlike the definitive and clearly formed notions that boys convey, girls are more comfortable with a more ambiguous God.

Girls seem to be less power-oriented and are inclined to discuss the Deity's role in relationships and interpersonal affairs. They may be interested in world problems and war and peace, but their imagery is usually not as graphic and aggressive as the imagery of boys. Girls sometimes express a desire to be God's partner and are much more open to the idea of a female God. Some girls may insist that God is female, or as Andrew Greeley describes in his autobiography, girls are more receptive to "the womanliness of God." You may ask your daughter, "Would the world be different if everyone believed that God was a woman? How?" Then you can share your own views of this increasingly controversial subject. What do you and your spouse believe?

For both sexes, there is still a great deal of uncertainty about God's gender—or if God even has one! It is a volatile area for family discussion, but most revealing about how men and women are perceived in our society. In discussing God and gender with your child, keep in mind that some children think that God is a little of both sexes. Twelve-year-old Lorraine expressed the following: "It could be God is beyond differences between boys and girls," she reflects, "but God also said we were made like God. I believe that God may have a little of both sexes but I'm afraid to say this out loud." Perhaps Lorraine is suggesting that we allow ourselves and our children more creative possibilities when it comes to God's gender and that we should not impose gender limitations on God—just as we would not want to unwisely limit our children in other ways.

How Can You Discover More About Your Child's God Image?

When asking your child about his or her notion of God, be sure to proceed with care and sensitivity. Sometimes children prefer to keep certain notions and beliefs private. As a good parent, it is imperative that you always respect your child's wishes.

You may find it helpful to divide your discussion into God's physical characteristics and God's psychological qualities. Ordinarily, it is easier for children to talk about physical details first; that serves as a good warm-up for the more intricate description of God's habits and motives.

Not all children imagine God in a physical way but most certainly do. Our society is so visual that children's imagery is probably more vivid now than it was in the past. Children seem to form a global impression of God initially, determined by size and visibility.

If you ask your youngster to draw a picture, assure your child that a Picasso drawing is not expected. What's inside a person and how a person expresses things is what really matters. Make certain that you distinguish this from a school assignment. That means no grades, no evaluations, and no parents' dirty looks! Simply explain that you want to know how your child pictures God.

Begin by letting your child draw alone for ten or fifteen minutes. If you furnish your youngster with a large assortment of crayons, you should return to a God figure that has come to life. Be sure not to unintentionally influence what your child draws or cue your child about what to include. Once, while I was talking with a seven-year-old girl about

God, her mother started playing religious songs like "You Light Up My Life" on the stereo in the next room. Musical accompaniment can be soothing, but it can also shape your child's mood and thinking.

When you first look at your youngster's drawing, respond by letting your child know that you appreciate or admire the drawing. Looking closely at some of the characteristics will help you better understand his or her ideas. Is God big or small? Does God look like a human being? What color and shape is God? Does God have a face? What expression does it have? Is God clear, or distant and mysterious? Is God alone in the drawing?

The main purposes of the drawing exercise are to develop your child's thinking about God and to help you better appreciate how comfortable your child is with the idea of God. If used judiciously, drawings can reveal a great deal about a child's attitude toward formal religion, their sense of trust in the world, how close he or she feels to God, and their feelings of self-esteem. More importantly, your child's drawings can disclose hidden aspirations, fears, and preoccupations that your child may harbor. An elaborate drawing can tell you much about how your child views the world.

Not all children's drawings are created equal. Some children attach hands and legs to a torso and emphasize God's human characteristics. Children also like to place their own trademark on the figure, such as a pipe borrowed from their image of dad or a baseball bat borrowed from some left-handed slugger. Some that I have uncovered are more graphic and unconventional:

In his comical drawing, Bob demonstrates that he thinks about God in terms of familiar media characters like

Bob, age 6½

Bugs Bunny. Apparently, Christianity and the Crucifixion in particular have been pervasive themes in Bob's family, and Bob is in the process of understanding the role of Jesus Christ. But the imagery is not fully comprehended. Bob seems to find the vision of a man on a cross too noxious an image. The notion of suffering, even for a good cause, is more than Bob can bear at this age. The formal imagery concerning Jesus was too heavy and negative for him.

Thus, in contrast to the teaching of formal Catholicism, Bob replaces Jesus with the happy-go-lucky figure of Bugs. By choosing an animal rather than a human being, Bob distances himself from the painful suffering. By choosing a popular comic character, Bob adds joviality and lightheartedness to a dark situation. Bob is trying to reject formal notions of God because he may feel uncomfortable with their somber nature. Yet, he retains the cross in his drawing—so his wandering away from religious teachings is perhaps temporary.

To facilitate your understanding, and to explore your child's thoughts further, I recommend an additional technique. If your child has already drawn a picture, and if the drawing is sufficiently detailed and involved, ask your child to think up a story about the picture. Again, assure your child that the story does not have to be complicated. Just encourage your child to follow his thoughts.

To assist your child in constructing a story, you can offer the following questions:

> What's going on in the story?
> What is God thinking and feeling?
> What will God do next?
> Does the story have an ending?
> What are the story's other characters feeling?

These questions provide a convenient and comforting sense of structure for your child's story and will help your child organize his or her thoughts. Your child's answers will reveal his or her feelings about God. If your child fears

God, these questions may highlight the reasons for that trepidation. If your child loves God, that significant experience can emerge as well. This technique is bound to make you add dimension to your child's spiritual world.

In order to best focus on God's presence, some parents encourage their children to pray and use prayer as a basic means of communication. If you and your spouse believe in the centrality of prayer in your child's life, then you should consider the following questions: Is prayer a structured ritual or a spontaneous expression of faith? Is your child using prayer to request things from God or as an expression of thankfulness? For some other special purpose? If your child already prays, try to discover what he or she prays about. Prayer can be the means by which you open up a dialogue about specific spiritual matters with your child.

You may also want to find out if—or how—your child believes that God hears and responds to prayer. This is important because it lets you know what your child thinks he or she is getting from praying. It can also help you guide your child's prayers so that they are more meaningful. Why does your child think that people pray? Is it only to ask God for things? Does your child think that God is always listening? What is the best way to get God's attention? Pay special attention to what your child thinks about the process of prayer; you might be surprised. A young woman I know tells the story of herself as a seven-year-old believing that you could make a long-distance phone call to God. "I used to pick up the receiver and have a chat," she remembers. "I figured it wouldn't cost much since my father worked for the phone company. Boy, was I disheartened when my father told me that we didn't get any special benefits. I figured I would try to talk to God in another way. So I started praying."

When it is performed in a heartfelt way, prayer can be a refreshing and creative opportunity for youngsters. As one seven-year-old named Andi said: "I like to pray because it helps me get out my feelings, and tell God how I feel. Sometimes it even helps me find answers and get along better with my sisters. I feel that God hears me when I pray to Him."

c⚡ 6

Discussing God's Role in the World

"God,
   What did Adam and Eve do for fun? My mom said they played with toys and ate, but I know better.

Chris
(age 9)"
FROM *DEAR GOD*

Children are very concerned with how God's presence manifests itself in the world around us. "Okay, so there's this great thing we can't see," they reason, "but how can we tell what It does on earth?" On one hand, children hear about some nebulous Deity that everyone seems to pray to. On the other hand, they see and read about wars, bad snowstorms, acts of cruelty, and acts of charity. How can you reconcile all these occurrences with the God that you believe in? And, how can you communicate that to your child? Children want to know more about God in words and ideas that they can understand. Real-life events provide the best sources for discussions about God.

Religious leaders are ordinarily better trained in philosophy and theology than in psychology. So it is not always easy for them to offer practical advice. Beyond that, if God is truly unknowable and indescribable, then even our best attempts at example and metaphor will necessarily fall short.

We all share in the dilemma of how to understand God's presence in our world and apply that to our lives. So take comfort in knowing that you are not alone as a parent. Looking for God is like searching for a white pearl in the snow. You know it is there somewhere, but it blends in so perfectly with the scenery that it is difficult to grasp.

It is a good deed and a wise parental decision to try to talk to your child about God's appearance in the world. If you want your child to accept God into his or her life, then God must have practical and lasting significance for him. In other words, God must be relevant!

Discussing the Mystery of God

Seven-year-old Tony, a Catholic youngster who professes a good deal of faith, has been heard to say, "I can't see God but I know He's there because my Mom said He was." Eight-year-old Kirk, raised in an agnostic family with Catholic roots, candidly acknowledges his skepticism about God. "Why should I believe in God when I can't see anything or hear anything at all?" is Kirk's blunt question. For thousands of children, the mystery and invisibility of God and the lack of a tangible appearance is quite troublesome. Kirk's father describes the difficulty for parents: "You teach your kid to test things out and prove them—in science, in sports, in anything—so religion just goes against the grain."

We all know that it is difficult to teach a child about intangible concepts. But does that mean that children cannot grasp the notion of God? We teach them about abstract concepts like liberty and honesty, so some communication about intangibility is possible. We teach them about historical figures like George Washington and Abraham Lincoln, so some appreciation for characters from the past is clearly tenable. While God, an invisible Being, may be more mysterious, He *can* be understood by the vast majority of children—particularly once they reach seven or eight years of age.

What can you say to help your child with the mystery of God? Because it is so difficult this topic requires more structured guidance from you rather than a great deal of questioning. You can ask your child why he or she thinks God is a mystery, but don't anticipate an elaborate response. The subject is too complex.

When speaking about God's mystery, consider all the things that you and your child feel are ambiguous about God. Five- and six-year-olds may be most interested in why God cannot be seen, but older children may have other pressing concerns. They may wish to know if God is truly all-powerful and all-knowing. "Does God know my thoughts?" they may wonder. An eleven-year-old who spends considerable time alone may wonder why God is so silent. So it is important for you to be prepared to answer your child's wide range of questions about God's mystery.

Some parents respond to their children by acknowledging their own uncertainty about the mystery of God. That reaction is certainly fine if it allows parent and child to explore together. Other parents try to offer an answer or an exploration for their children's questions. They might say that God hears a person's prayers and needs even though that person is not aware of it at the time. They might add that as a person gets older, he can see that God is there with him because he has more experiences in which God has helped him. Always feel free to offer your personal philosophy and understanding of God, but also allow your child to express his or her ideas.

Consider the possible relationships between mystery and faith. Perhaps you also feel that God's mystery builds faith or inspires faith in people. Or you may have no idea why God is mysterious but you find yourself having no less belief in God. Could God remain somewhat mysterious in order to leave room for human faith, one of our most basic human experiences? It is an interesting and provocative notion for sure, but one among many possible explanations. Don't be afraid to discuss any possibility with your child. Such a discussion may open up a dialogue about how close or distant your child perceives God to be.

When you sense a readiness in your youngster, proceed to the question of how God is revealed in the world if God can't be seen. What forms may God assume? What are the Lord's most accessible roles and who are the Lord's messengers? Briefly outline for your child how you think he or she might be able to recognize God. Consider a variety of alternatives: in nature, in church or synagogue, in friends and relatives, in you and your spouse, and in themselves. Suggest to your youngster what it means to feel God's presence. For example, ask your child to remember a time that he or she wished for something really hard and it came true. Then ask your child to focus on the feeling of thankfulness in relation to God's role. If your child responds to this example, continue by asking, "Where else can you find God's presence?"

Throughout your discussion of God's mystery, remember that this subject is truly among the most difficult of theological topics. It is particularly hard for children to digest and for parents to help them with. So be patient. A child who is not ready for the question of God's mystery at age six may well be curious and animated about "this invisible God" by age eight.

Talking to Your Child About Creation

Ted, a forty-year-old Lutheran parent, related the following story taken from a conversation with his nine-year-old daughter, Lorna. Lorna had been learning about the Bible in religious school, and Ted was wondering how she liked school.

"She asked me if I ever heard of a woman named Eve who was married to a guy named Adam," Ted reported about his daughter. "I told her their names rang a bell. Lorna went on to say that she thought it was wrong for Eve to get a bad image, and that everybody should get a second chance. She wanted to know why God made the tree and the snake in the first place. (Pause.) Sometimes kids are curious about some things that are hard to explain."

Talking about Creation is useful because it can serve as a natural lead-in to other interesting topics about religion. Sometimes, as Ted discovered, children are openly curious about the origin of things. Other children may be less visibly intrigued, so it may require a bit more conversation and patience on your part.

If you were Ted, and your daughter made a similar comment about the Genesis story, what would you say?

First you might ask your child for his or her impressions about the Creation story. Do not react to your child as if his or her notions are right or wrong. Instead, try to accept your child's ideas for what they are: one child's interpretation.

If your child is skeptical about a learned account, ask why. Was there anything in particular about the story that your child doubts? Was it the way Adam and Eve were created? The number of days that Creation took? Was it the talking, tempting serpent? Tell your child your beliefs and explain how you agree or disagree with traditional versions of Creation. Make certain to present yourself not only as a parent, but as an individual with his or her own ideas.

Some parents choose to speak about Creation in terms of God's love for mankind. What did God give to people at the outset? What did God decide that people must work for? What does all this say about the nature of God's love for us? Come to some conclusions for yourself and then share them with your youngster.

For example, you may wish to say: "God gave us life and that is the best gift of all, better than the biggest Christmas present!" Or you may decide to explain to your child, "God's love for mankind is expressed through the beauty of nature, like bright red tulips, the ocean that we love to swim in, beautiful animals, and the birds that chirp every morning." Whatever you choose to communicate, real-life examples will help your child imagine God's creative touch.

Creation may also bring to mind something nearly all

children are curious about. How babies are born. We have learned from the seminal studies of Jean Piaget and other developmental psychologists that children are in fact fascinated by their origins and the circumstances of their siblings' births. Children often ask about babies even before they begin school, especially if they have a younger brother or sister. Ask yourself first how the creation of the earth might have been like giving birth to a child. That can lead you to discuss Genesis, Adam and Eve, innocence, original sin, or whatever you believe.

You can also compare the original act of Creation with forms of creativity accessible and familiar to your child. What does God's creative inspiration have to do with a child's drawing, block building, clay formations or musical compositions? Try to encourage your child to consider what he or she goes through in creating something new. What is it like to stare at a blank sheet of paper and then place colors upon it to make a work of art? What is it like to listen to silence and then sing a song? Or even to make a horn with a paper towel cylinder? Your child knows about these creative activities; therefore, he or she can think about Creation too. You may wish to say that the greatest wonder of creativity is that everything has a purpose and a place— everything goes together in harmony. God's greatness is more than a spiritual mandate; it is evidenced by the orderliness of natural things in the world. For example, the sun rises every day and the seasons appear in order every year! So talk to your child about Creation with confidence and enthusiasm and relate the origin of life to common events that occur in his or her life. The way you speak with your child will be an act of creation itself, if you follow your heart and leap into hard-to-understand questions.

While no one—neither the scientist nor the theologian—can be sure about the precise time and place of Creation, we are all entitled to an opinion. Too often we prematurely limit our ideas about Creation. Don't do that with your youngster. Here are a few ideas that may help you in discussing Creation with your child.

Ideas About Creation

1. We don't know if Creation was easy for God! What do *you* think?
2. Do you think things began in Asia, Africa, Atlantis, Atlanta, or where?
3. We don't know if Earth was God's only creative project! What else do you think He might have created?
4. We don't know why God rested! Do you think God gets tired?
5. We don't know what six days meant in those days! Could one day then have been what we call a year?
6. We don't know if apples were apples in those days! Could Eve have taken a bite from another kind of food? What, for instance?
7. If there was an Adam and Eve, we don't know what Adam was doing when Eve was tempted by the serpent! What do you suppose he was doing?

What Does God Have to Do With War and Peace?

The most poignant portrait of God that I know about occurs in the Bible's Exodus. In that chapter the reader learns about God's opinion of war and destruction. As the vengeful Egyptians are drowning in the sea, God becomes upset with the Jews. A distressed God appeals to their humanity, as He mourns the mass slaughter of their pursuers—also children of God. "Why do you rejoice when my children are dying?" God laments. Whether or not you accept that historical account, the principles involved are most interesting. A Deity who does not desire tranquility for us has no basis for existence. A God who yearns for our peace on Earth is well worth considering—particularly as you speak with your child.

Children harbor all kinds of ideas about God's role in the cataclysmic events of the world, and not all their notions are hopeful and benign. While discussing God's activities, children sometimes mention war spontaneously. For example, six-year-old Gerard had this to say about the violence he sees in the world.

"God is a fighting force," Gerard said. "The president and God had a war, and they used weapons like swords and chains. God just has wars. They're going around all over the world. We have to fight them for Him. Even the president."

Gerard's aggressive depiction is more extreme than most children's ideas, but many other youngsters wonder about why God allows wars to continue. Has your son or daughter asked about God's role in war? If not, ask them what they think of these conflicts in light of God.

What will you say to your child about God's role in world affairs? Does God do all that is possible? Do you wonder why God doesn't help more? Use concrete and specific events in your discussion of international circumstances or simply respond to your child's questions. Look for questions like: "Mom, why is there war if God is good?" Such questions let you know that your child is eager for a frank discussion.

It is crucial to be as honest as possible when it comes to your views. Don't pretend to possess all the answers. But don't feign ignorance either, for you have a wealth of life experience to draw upon—use it! For example, you might say to your child: "War is awful. When I was just a little older than you, our country was at war in Vietnam. It was terrible, and many innocent people were killed. We have to learn to get along with other people, and we have to keep trying. God is there in our persistent efforts to love and stop war, even if we don't always understand how He works."

The second important thing to remember is not to paint an overly bleak or falsely rosy picture of the world. Acknowledge that there is horrible violence in the world, but stress examples of peace and beauty too. Discuss God's involvement throughout. Talk about who may be responsible for world problems but also who is behind works of art, the Grand Canyon, or a sunset. Keep your conversations about the world balanced between things that are uplifting and positive and things that are more disconcerting. What is God responsible for and what should be attributed to mankind?

What kinds of things can a parent say about God and the subject of war? You must listen closely to your own conscience. It may be helpful, however, to learn about what other parents say to their children. Here are some of the approaches I have observed parents use with their children.

Communicating About God and War

1. Tell your child that God can only prevent fighting if people are willing to cooperate.

2. Suggest that not everyone in the world has truly discovered God yet. For if they did, there would be no more wars.
3. Emphasize that God doesn't cause war and therefore feels that it is wrong to intervene. It is up to those who start a war to halt its terrible effect.
4. Speculate that a particular war may be furthering the cause of peace in the long run. Introduce the notion that God sometimes acts in strange and unusual ways.
5. Suggest that it is not God who is involved in war, but evil forces like greed, selfishness, and hatred that are at work. Sin may not be omnipotent like God, but it may be forceful and persistent in its own right. And all of us are capable of sin. Be careful not to frighten your child with the idea of sin.

Try to buffer your child by reassuring him or her that sin does not win out in the end, but it must be confronted. Emphasize the inevitability of God's beneficent presence in the world.

Remember that you are not just having a minor chat with your child when you speak about war, you are advocating a certain view of the world and even a perspective on the universe. So be thorough and sensitive, and encourage your child to express himself and his questions freely.

Consider the advice of fifty-three-year-old Peter, an Episcopalian father of four. Concerning his conversations over the years with his children, Peter recounts what he has learned.

"When they were young, I used to say a lot of flippant things about the world," Peter acknowledged. "I talked about what a mess we got ourselves into in Vietnam. I'd say

'For Christ sakes there ain't no God there.' Now I wish I had been more careful about what I said, or took the time to explain what I meant. The kids, especially the boys, picked up things I said and took it word for word."

Why Is There Suffering?

What follows naturally from talking about war and destruction is the subject of human suffering. Children wonder why people get hurt, why grandma or grandpa died, and why people are sometimes mean to each other, and they look to their parents for answers.

What did you say to your child the first time he or she skinned a knee or painfully bruised an elbow? Perhaps it was possible to attribute responsibility in those cases to your child's carelessness or rough play. But sometimes there seems to be no one to blame. What can we say under those circumstances, or when more serious suffering occurs because of injury, maltreatment, or hunger?

As they get older, children are increasingly intrigued by God's role in pain simply because they have experienced more of it. They want to know why it exists. By the time a child is eight or nine at the latest, and earlier for children with younger siblings, he or she knows about pain, injury, or displacement firsthand. By this age, children are quite aware that not all things in life are tailored for their needs, nor is all pain immediately relieved. As they become more attentive to the media, children begin to realize that there is also considerable suffering in the world around them.

Use your child's almost inevitable curiosity about

mundane injuries to talk to him or her about God. Allow yourself to rely upon established religious tenets as well as your own ideas.

It is usually wise to elicit your child's understanding of injury and pain at the outset. You don't want your child to be blaming himself or herself needlessly or secretly harboring some resentment toward you. You also do not want your child to believe the world is a frightening, unsafe place, even as you caution your child about dangerous risks and situations to avoid. You can probably accomplish what you want to by beginning with: "Why do you think you got hurt just now?" or "What could have caused your friend to get so sick?"

In helping your child understand pain, you must help your child sort out which negative events involve God and which do not if you believe it is possible for events to occur outside of God's scope. You should discuss whether some accidents just occur, or whether every circumstance or event has a reason. Be certain to take as clear a stance as you feel comfortable with, and remember to always elicit your child's reaction. Do accidents happen randomly? Do injuries happen arbitrarily? These are questions you can ponder honestly with your child.

Once you've discussed the realm of incidents that may involve God, you should switch hats and discuss those things that God doesn't participate in. For example, you may feel that an auto crash happens independently of God but a death by natural causes does not. Therefore, you will want to talk about your religious interpretations of naturally occurring death.

What is God's role in suffering then? As clearly as possible, tell your child whether you believe that God is an active participant or a passive bystander in human suffering. Tell him whether God can or cannot prevent suffering. Explain how God comforts. Is suffering an isolated occurrence, or an event related to an intricate set of events centered around God? Ultimately, you should talk to your child about whether God accomplishes some divine purpose through human suffering. In doing that, you can also talk about whether pain or injury brings about growth. You might say that pain is one way that we learn about our vulnerability and about our need for God and other people. Pain may teach us about goodness and compassion too, for it compels us to reach out and help or be helped by others. It also teaches us patience and to appreciate good health.

When discussing matters of suffering and pain, be sure to comfort your child often, especially at the conclusion of your talk. No conversation is worth upsetting your child or causing unnecessary tension. Make certain that your child is not unduly worried or pessimistic about suffering. Be sure that something has not gotten lost in the translation. You do not want your youngster to be fearful of God or afraid of life.

Even if you are very clear about your own beliefs, expect some confusion and misgivings on the part of your child, who will want to find his or her own answers, or combine your view with his own experiences. That means you've done your parenting job well, for you have set your child on a spiritual course of questioning and a search for the truth.

God, Science, and Nature

From the time children learn to appreciate nature to the time they must complete their first science fair project, children are encouraged to wonder about the origin of things. Who made the sunshine? Why does it rain? How did trees first grow? These are fundamental questions that children have been asking for generations. Can we make a computer to find out about the beginning of time? Can they make life in a test tube? These are the contemporary questions that can be added to the list.

About Science

"My son asks a lot of questions about the solar system and about our rocket capacity," says forty-three-year-old Thomas. "He thinks these scientific things have something to do with God too. That's pretty heavy stuff for an eight-year-old," Thomas adds with pride. "I wish I knew what to tell him."

Like Thomas, you too may encounter some difficult natural and scientific questions from your child. Some of your child's curiosities may explicitly involve God; others may implicitly suggest God's involvement. Since most of us do not have the credentials of Carl Sagan, we need to consider these questions in our own religious terms.

If your child asks you whether science can account for some of the things we attribute to God, what would you say? Perhaps we have merely evolved from other beings and Earth is an incredible consequence of stars colliding, or perhaps God is at the helm of our universe, having created all things.

You can tell your child that he or she is asking a good question, one which has perplexed many astronomers, physicists, and theologians. First, find out if your child has discussed the topic in school and whether his or her teacher offered an opinion. After discussing it, then proceed to your own views.

You can point out that science and God are potentially compatible, that one does not necessarily negate the other. For example, it is possible that God created the animals from whom mankind may have evolved; God also may have created the stars billions of years ago. The key thing to emphasize is: there must have been a purpose or an origin from which all other things developed. Encourage your child to keep learning about scientific discoveries and religious beliefs, and encourage him or her to question how ideas from the two fit together.

You can also stimulate your child's interest by looking for movies and public television shows which address scientific and religious questions. Sometimes an especially well-documented religious show is an excellent choice. There's an old movie that is one of the most provocative presentations of the evolution controversy. It's called *Inherit the Wind* and features Spencer Tracy and Gene Kelly. It's about the 1925 Scopes trial, which focused on a young teacher's right to teach evolution in the public school. The debates over religious belief and scientific knowledge are absorbing and the movie also reflects that period of American history. The movie is often shown on television or can probably be rented at your video store or library.

Whether you are just discussing science and religion or watching a program, keep alert to how your child is processing the two. Too many children that I have spoken with see science and religion as mutually exclusive. They see science and religion as competing for people's beliefs. For instance, Ken, a ten-year-old, writes in his letter to God:

"Dear God,
   I don't believe all that baloney my science teacher talks
about. The heck (excuse me) with big bangs and light
years. You're still the best.

                              Love,
                              Ken"
                              FROM PRIVATE COLLECTION

For the sake of Ken and other ten-year-olds like him,
a parent can offer some clarification that can save a lot of
confusion. I would recommend that you make a point of
distinguishing between fact and faith with your child.

   Remember that *fact* refers to an event or item that we
have shared knowledge and evidence for, including a scientific, historical, or even a metaphysical phenomenon. On
the other hand, *faith* refers to a conscious choice made by
a person or a group in the face of ambiguity. Faith is an
elective statement which frequently concerns religious matters and the way the world works. The existence of rainbows is a fact, but a story about their symbolic meaning is
a matter of faith. For example, if you said that rainbows are
God's sign that the world will never again be destroyed by
flood, or perhaps this is how God introduced color to the
world, these are notions based on faith, not fact.

   Tell your child that science is concerned with a limited,
finite number of facts that can be proven. Emphasize that
God exists in the realm of faith, which is an infinite area
that cannot be proved or disproved by scientific research.
Facts do help us understand things better, but we need
more than science to get closer to God. Ask your child,
"How else can we look for God?"

About Nature

You probably won't need to ask penetrating questions to get your child talking about nature. Children are frequently much more in touch with nature than adults, and their curiosity springs effortlessly from their ready awareness. Children may not always associate nature with God and religion.

If you choose to stimulate discussion with your child, there's a lighthearted way to organize your talks about nature. Invite your child on a field trip to a park or scenic area. Once you arrive, ask your child to think about the four seasons and speculate how God's presence may be manifested in each. Or ask him or her to choose a favorite aspect of each season and think about it. Consider how good it tastes or sounds or smells. Maybe your child will imagine a running brook in June or a mountain of snow in December. Perhaps your child has never thought of God in these ways before; encourage him to stop and think about God's role in nature more often.

This technique is especially popular with young children and is most vivid when the season at hand is considered. Winter, spring, summer, or fall—God is evident, and all we have to do is allow ourselves to look. Instilling the belief that God is everywhere we look will be a great comfort for your child, both now and as the years go by, as your child's life gets more complicated.

Your child will also be curious about some hard-to-explain things about nature. Perhaps he wonders what makes hurricanes, earthquakes, and other natural disasters happen. Listen for questions about such matters. Try to offer your child comforting explanations. Do you believe these events are acts of God? Or are these disasters events that make God sad too? Be clear and direct with your child, and the topic can stimulate a useful discussion that draws on the notion of God and "bad things."

Older children may prefer more of a question-and-answer approach when it comes to nature. Most older children, the nine- to twelve-year-olds, like to show off how much they know. Here are some challenging questions that you can ask and let them "show off" their wisdom:

QUESTIONS ABOUT NATURE

1. Did God make rivers?
2. Why do you think God made four seasons?
3. Do you think God has a favorite season? Which one? Why or why not? What's your favorite season?
4. Does God have anything to do with the leaves changing color? What? What parallels can you draw in terms of people changing?
5. How is a flower like a person?
6. When did you first see a rainbow? Where? What was it like?
7. Does God have anything to do with hurricanes? Volcanoes?
8. Does God have anything to do with fruits and vegetables?
9. Why do we say a blessing before meals?
10. What spiritual purpose could the ocean serve? Did God make the ocean? How do you know?

These questions should set your children thinking for a while!

What Does God Have to Do With Sexuality and Love?

This topic may be as pertinent for parents as individuals as it is for them as caretakers of their children. Sexuality and religion are too often segregated by many cultures and religions. Many of us grow up believing that religious ideas and sexual experiences have nothing to do with each other, or worse, that the two experiences invariably collide. We repress our sexuality in order to be religious or repress our notions of God in order to be freely sexual. Regrettably, we pass along these expectations to our children as we teach them about their minds and bodies.

So I would highly recommend taking the initiative and talking to your older children about what God has to do with his or her sexual development. Use your own judgment regarding your individual child, although many youngsters are ready by age ten or eleven. You can begin by suggesting to your child that his or her body is a gift from God that is to be loved and cared for. Emphasize that the body is as much a spiritual part of your child as his or her mind or heart.

Note your child's reactions. Is this new information for your child? Is he or she comfortable hearing about sexuality and religion from you? These are questions to keep in mind that can prompt a discussion of specific topics such as breast development, menstruation, and puberty.

According to Helen, a thirty-seven-year-old Methodist mother: "It's not that I don't wonder about my religious beliefs and love and sex, it's, well, I'm not sure whether I should say something to my kids," Helen explains.

"They're beginning to ask about things—about conception and differences between boys and girls—and I try to tell them about values, but I'm afraid I don't clearly say what I mean."

What does God have to do with a person's sexuality? Or their ability to love? Ask your older child to think about sexuality and love as part of his or her personality, like intelligence or kindness. Suggest that when the time is right, God must want us to enjoy sexuality as much as other things in life. Perhaps we are experiencing another gift from God when we are developing sexually, and sexual feelings arise along with the caring and thoughtfulness associated with the opposite sex. That's one reason why adults sometimes have sex in order to have children—to experience the wonderment of God through the birth of a baby.

Ask your child if he or she has thought much about how babies are born, and ask if God is involved. See if you can detect what your child's fantasies about birth are. This can be an excellent way of curtailing any confusions about sex early on.

When it comes to speaking about caution in sexual matters, be careful not to be dogmatic or preachy. Remember that any useful religious standards for sex are neither overly permissive nor overly prohibitive. You want to communicate a view of sexuality that is consistent with your view of God, but above all, you want to express a view that is in line with your child's happiness and welfare.

Your ten- or eleven-year-old may wonder how your feelings for your spouse differ from your parental love. Your child may wonder at a given moment: "Do you love me too?" When you respond to your child's concerns, remember that all love stems from divine love. Genuine parental love or marital love are forms of divine love, expressed toward a particular person. Remember that divine love is expansive and limitless; it encompasses all of our world and can be manifest in many ways—showing love toward a friend, neighbor, grandparent, or even a pet. Assure your child that although your love for him or her is different from the sexual love you feel toward your spouse, your love for your child is just as strong. Reinforce that message with nurturance and you will have communicated a great deal about God, love, and sexuality.

How May God Be Manifested in Your Family?

Sometimes we look for God only in exotic or faraway places. Teach your child about God's emergence in our world. Remember to conclude any such discussion with God's relationship to your family. Consider the ways in which God emerges in your everyday routine.

What does God have to do with the food you serve your child? Some theologians believe that food is in itself a spiritual entity. That's why some religions encourage grace before and after meals. That's also why some religions offer so much important imagery surrounding food, like bread and wine in many Christian religions.

Partaking of food is an experience you share each day with your child, so make it an event that includes spiritual awareness. Make your child's favorite meal or dessert, and ask your child to stop and think about where food originally comes from. Can it be considered a gift from God? If so, it makes sense to take a minute to thank God for food; for parents who provide it; for a healthy body that uses it for strength to run and play. Tell him how it feels to care for him by preparing the food you place on the table. Let him know that the hours of shopping, preparation, and serving are all just one more way that you say "I love you" to your child.

Marie, a twenty-nine-year-old Catholic mother, talks about the role of nurturing her family. "When I make pancakes with natural maple syrup in the morning," Marie began, "and I see the smile on my daughter's face, I feel really warm inside. I know that just as my child is a gift from God, I feel that I can nourish her through preparing food with love. It just feels good to make her happy and to share in God's love in this simple way." Consider the role of food at festivals and family gatherings. Think about the special focus on food at Thanksgiving or during the holiday season. Ask your child to consider how food, as a gift from God, helps to gather your family together, brings you closer together in spirit, and serves as a bond between God and his people.

Any conversation about God's presence in the family will lead to the relationships you have with each other. That's really what this entire book is about: The essence of God in your family is the way you and your child express love and respect. So suggest to your youngster that God arises in the love and affection you have for each other, and in the camaraderie that friends and family members share. Point out that God is manifested when we care about each other's needs, both at happy times and sad times; like comforting a friend who didn't make the team, or being excited for a friend who gets to go to Disneyland or receives a great new toy.

Also present a good number of family circumstances in which you believe God appears. Perhaps your child has a dog or cat that is special and treated like a member of the family. Ask your child to think about his or her affection for the pet. What can your child do to more completely treat the pet with love? Why is that important to God? Your goal can be to instill a sense of responsibility in your child when it comes to the pet's care, and you can also use the situation to teach a spiritual lesson about love.

Forty-year-old Wayne, father of three and owner of one dog, Dookie, explained: "If your kids don't treat a pet with kindness, then they shouldn't have one. I tell my kids that Dook is like a permanent guest. We must care for Dookie like we would a relative, with hospitality and love. Christ teaches us to be kind to animals as well as people."

What ideas does your child have about how God is expressed in your family? Does your child ever feel an absence of God? At what time? Does that troublesome feeling still linger? Talking about your family and God can also be a time for healing.

Keep your conversation balanced. Talk to your child about family strengths and family weaknesses, about joyous occasions and somber ones. Discuss events that stand out, such as graduations or confirmations, and your everyday routine as well: Parent-child relations, sibling love and rivalry, and grandparents, too. Throughout, remember that God is the common denominator in your discussion and that respect for the God in every individual, from ages five to ninety-five, is paramount.

I am reminded of a poem I received from a woman

named Nancy who presents puppet shows for children. One of her star puppets is very wise when it comes to religious matters and the family. During the shows, the little cloth doll, wearing children's clothes, reminds the audience where to look for God:

> God is everyone that you'll ever know
> God is everything that you'll ever see
> The spirit in you
> The spirit in me.

The poem can apply to your family too. Look for the spirit of God in your family and encourage your child to do likewise.

PART THREE

*HELPING YOUR
CHILD
FIND GOD*

Discussing the Nature and Purpose of Religion

"Dear God,
I know that you are made of all kinds of people. When I suggested this in religious school my teacher told me I was wrong.
You should be more careful about who you hire to teach your stuff.

Yours truly,
Marci
(age 11)"
FROM PRIVATE COLLECTION

Some parents prefer to speak about God without reference to a specific religion. Disenchanted with established religions or brought up without strong religion themselves, these parents want to concentrate on a fresh view of God separate from tradition.

Other parents feel differently. Dedicated to a particular belief system and reared in the ambience and customs of that system, these parents wish to pass along a historical understanding to their children. Or choosing a newfound religion as their own, parents may take the traditions and beliefs to heart and wish to communicate them to their children. Religion then becomes an integral part of family life.

Whichever your attitude about formal religion, or even if you have ambivalent feelings about your religion of birth, it is important for you to talk to your child about religion as well as about God.

"A kid grows up and hears about Jews, Buddhists, Arabs and wants to know what it all means," says forty-two-year-old Robert, a Baptist father of four. "Even if you don't think too much of religion yourself, you have to help them sort it all out."

That's the first reason to discuss religion with your child. Your child will naturally encounter a tremendous amount of information about religions, and will require some guidance in understanding them. Your child will also meet many people with different religious views. How can your child appreciate them without a solid grounding in religion?

A second reason to discuss religion is so that you convey a belief system to your child, whether or not you are identified formally with a particular denomination. In the things you say or do with your child, you are conveying a distinct view of life and death. Sometimes you may even express a *cosmology*, a view of the origin of things. This happens, for example, when you speak about the weather or about the cause of certain events. For most parents, what is actually communicated to a child is a combination of formal religious beliefs and a parent's interpretation of those beliefs. For others, it's a combination of these religious beliefs and their individual opinions.

The third reason for preparing to discuss religion with your child is to distinguish the notion of God from the worship of God, which is what most religions are about. Your child, or anyone for that matter, may have a concept of God that is aligned with established notions of God—but it also may be very unconventional. It is important to communicate that an individual can believe in God in his or her own way, not matter how much that image differs from other people's representations. Emphasize to your child that by establishing his or her own image of God, he or she will become a complete and more mature person.

What Does Religion Have to Do With It, Anyway?

When your child first begins to hear about God and then learns about religions, he or she may wonder how the two go together. "Okay, so there's this thing that started everything," your child may reason, "but why do people light candles and make colored glass windows because of it?"

The answer to that question is not as straightforward as it might seem. It requires you to think deeply about why you are observant or why not, and why you believe deeply in God or do not.

When your child picks up details about rituals and beliefs in Sunday school, during a religious service, or at home, the process is similar to the way he or she learns at school. Your child will sift through religious symbolism, images of Old Testament battles, bread and wine, or holy water, and retain those images or ideas that stand out. The symbols of formal religion may become part of your child through habit or even as belief, but they are not easily connected with ideas about a living God.

God often remains an enigma, or an entity who is separate from religious practices. Your child needs to relate God and religion if you are going to make religious affiliation meaningful. It is your responsibility as parent to facilitate that relationship of ideas. You must answer the question, "What does religion have to do with God, anyway?"

In practical terms, you need to explain why religion is relevant for your child. If you want your child to follow the tenets of a particular religion, like Catholicism or Protestantism, then you need to delineate why those ideas are relevant to your child. And if you want your child to emulate your own personal religious ideas, independent of formal religious belief, then again you must explain why your beliefs are relevant to the life of your child. There is no other way to seriously pass along religion to your child. For instance, you might explain that a belief in God similar to yours will help him or her through rough or lonely times. Use an example or two from your own life, perhaps a time when you had to move and leave all of your friends and were scared of meeting all new kids. Perhaps your faith in God was instrumental in getting used to your new town, home, and school.

You can also describe how in ancient times people developed religions to make sense of the natural things they observed, as well as the supernatural things. Many of the early primitive religions were focused upon the sun, the moon, and the stars. The Egyptians and the Greeks believed that there were many specialized gods who ruled over specific natural phenomena: a sun god, a god for fire, a moon god for love and wisdom, etc. First with the advent of Judaism, and later with the emergence of Christianity, the notion of a single God became a matter of ardent belief and controversy. Some people believe that this notion was a matter of divine inspiration; others believe that it was an illustration of mankind's development.

You can tell your child that most modern ideas about religion are derived from these two approaches to life. A religion is an organized system of beliefs and rituals which centers on a supernatural being (usually God), and it is a way of thought embraced with zeal and devotion. But also explain about religion in a child's terms. You can say that it is one way people form a community or a group because they believe in the same ideas. Ten-year-old Fred, a Lutheran child, believes that "A religion is something you have because it gives you a chance to see all the other people and keep in touch with them. That way you can talk and get closer and find out how much you are alike and how much you want the same things for your families."

You can then discuss with your child what it means to be religious. First ask your child what he or she thinks of being a religious person means. Add that being religious means adhering to a particular religion or religions. It means conscientiously following the beliefs of that religion in your own life. "Being religious," you can say, "is not just a matter of belonging, but a matter of practicing and acting." Remember to include what the boundaries are for being religious. You can tell your child, "A person can be religious but not be a member of a religious group; another person who *is* part of a religious group may *not* actually be religious." Being religious is more a part of how we treat other people—the way we'd want them to treat us—than joining a group.

"I don't go to church much, but I consider myself religious," says sixty-year-old Tom, who is a Catholic by birth and a father of four. "I believe in God about as much as anybody can, but my way of being religious is just to help people get along. I guess you could say I've formed my own religion as I've lived. I'm sure about God, but you have to organize your life around the things that really matter to you as a person. And stick to those beliefs."

Tom further explained that his four children, now grown, were curious, each in his own way, about religion. One child wanted to know, "What is God for?" Another child asked, "Why do we celebrate holidays?" The other two children were nearly identical in their questioning: "Why do people go to church every week?" These kinds of questions are common for children, particularly in the middle childhood years, ages seven to nine.

Has your child asked about the purpose of religion? What would you say? If you consider what seems to link most of the world's religions, they share a singular purpose of worshipping God. We have religion to recognize, worship, and celebrate God. Some of our children, brought up in a nation which stresses democratic principles and allegiance to no individual ruler, find the worship of God a bit disconcerting. After all, worship of God seems like adhering to a monarch, albeit an invisible, spiritual one. Try to distinguish for your child how a religion which revolves around God is different from a government that revolves around a monarch. Emphasize what you really believe about God. If you feel that worshipping God makes for a happier life, then say so. If you believe that revering God brings greater peace, then discuss that.

Most religions seem to advocate the worship of God in order to live a more coherent and fulfilled life. They urge that there is only one direction that matters in life, and that is the direction that brings a person closer to God. Religions may differ dramatically, however, in the ways they worship God. Everyone has his own idea about how best to worship God.

Your child will probably wonder about what other purposes religions have, besides the basic common interest of worshipping God. While this shared focus must be stressed, there are some other common purposes that many religions seem to demonstrate.

Many religions see one of their major purposes as answering questions about life. Due to life's ambiguity, both adults and children carry around perplexing questions about how to live and how to make moral choices. They want to know how to act in certain situations and how to deal with life's ups and downs. Religions can provide guidance in these matters, usually through the counsel or teaching of the clergy, and can often serve to explain God's ways to us. For example, when a boy or girl has questions about what God looks like, they can ask their priest, minister, or rabbi, as well as their parents.

Many religions help people maintain greater order in their lives. By advocating certain religious laws or patterns of conduct, such as dietary laws or annual schedules, religions can try to forge organization around important religious themes and beliefs. They can direct people toward health and well-being and provide a philosophical basis for many behaviors. You might tell your child that religions supply clarity and order. For example, religion can teach us that it is advisable and important to have a day of rest as well as to work hard.

Many religions see an additional purpose for belief— and that is to teach about God and significant historical figures. In order to worship God properly, these religions contend, we need to know about God and God's representations. Thus, some religions focus considerable attention on forefather figures like Abraham, Jesus, Elijah, and Buddha. Often these figures are exemplary because they illustrate how a person can be braver, stronger, happier, more honest, or more successful than they could have been without God. These figures are also teachers in the subject of God's presence and greatness. They can also teach us why we should worship God. Explain this to your child.

Numerous religious groups also emphasize peace as a primary function of religious belief. It is certainly a central aspect of Christian traditions, as well as Judaism, Hinduism, and Islam. Religions may disagree a great deal about how peace can be realized, but trusting in God is ordinarily a prerequisite. You should also teach your child that peace is a goal of many religions. Many religious traditions have formal prayers for peace, which ask God to use divine power to make people (and nations) get along better.

Most religions grow because members are looking for a sense of community based on shared values. Religions provide a formal house of worship or a designated meeting place for followers, even as early as biblical times. Religions frequently encourage people to pray together, often through singing or chanting. Over time religions can also foster a sense of camaraderie or religious brotherhood among members. So describe these elements to your child, whether or not you identify formally with a religious group. Why not ask, "Have you ever noticed people of a religious group full of this kind of spirit who seem to have a special, close relationship with each other? What do you think is special about it? Would it be the same if they were all members of a club? What's different about it?"

In order for your child to really appreciate what religions other than your own are about, it is helpful to provide a few illustrations. Talking about a few religions provides your child with a glimpse of what religions have in common, as well as how they differ. If you include some discussion of religions like Buddhism, which is not God-focused, or ways of thought that are even skeptical about God, your child can begin to see how systems of belief can diverge dramatically.

Discussing different religions without denigration also carries the spiritual message of religious tolerance to your child. The more aware your child is of the diversity that exists concerning beliefs about God, the less rigid his or her view of God will be. I also believe that if your child understands them in the larger world context, he or she is likely to be more sensitive to your own religious views.

While some children from ages four to six may not be very attentive to your descriptions of world religions, most older children will be if you present essential beliefs in a clear and interesting manner. A good way to broach the subject is to take one religion a week for several weeks and explore its major tenets. Whatever structure you employ, it is important to elicit your children's feedback along the way. Remember to ask, "Do you think some of those ideas are good or bad? Why? How is this religion different from ours, or different from the religious beliefs of grandma and grandpa?"

You can select any religions you prefer for discussion, or with older children, you may ask for a suggestion. "Is there any religion that you've heard about that you're particularly interested in?" you may ask your child.

Focus all discussions on what each religion has to say about God. By considering different concepts of God, your discussion will seem less like a school lesson and more like your previous talks about personal beliefs. You can also get to the central purpose of each religion very quickly, which should help facilitate discussion with your child.

Below are summary descriptions of a number of religions your child is likely to hear about at school or in the news. I have chosen a representative cross section of the world's religions. Please use these descriptions as a guide and inspiration for your talks; don't merely read the summaries to your child. Interact with your son or daughter and encourage questions and further exploration.

Because I will be outlining pragmatic information for America's three major religious groups in the chapter that follows, I have chosen to focus on other significant religions here. These religious traditions are: Hinduism, Islam, Buddhism, and Eastern Orthodoxy; and American religions, such as Quakerism, the Mormon Church, and Agnosticism.

What Is Hinduism?

If your child asks about this religion from India, or you want to bring up the subject in a prepared fashion, there are a number of distinguishing features and beliefs that you can highlight.

Hinduism goes back to about 1500 B.C., when it arose out of the philosophical exchanges of native beliefs and Western invader doctrines in India. The fundamental text, or "Bible," of Hinduism is the Veda, and includes descriptions of rituals, mythology, and philosophical commentary. Of great interest to many people in the West are the colorful and wise epic stories about gods and heroes included in this text.

You can discuss Hinduism's ideas about God. Hinduism stresses that there is only one Creator, though there may be many gods which are part of this single Creator. Hinduism stresses that everything in life goes together. All forms of life are part of the Divine, even if they may appear disconnected to us.

With regard to the human experience, Hindu thought observes that people go through a continuous cycle of birth and rebirth called samsara. Suggest that your child can relate to this notion by remembering the cycles of the seasons, ocean tides, and other patterns of nature. According to Hinduism, the repetition of the cycle is determined by the nature of our past acts, or a cumulative energy called karma. The goal of mankind is to achieve acts of great purity and to come back to Earth as a different, better-living being. Only with pure thoughts and pure devotion to the divine principle can peace be found.

Hinduism offers a great variety of private rituals and public devotions, including religious chanting. Puja, a ceremonial dinner for the Divine, is one of the most common. In the United States, Hindu thought has been spread by Indian immigrants and traveling teachers or gurus. Hindu beliefs are often accepted by many Americans, sometimes in conjunction with Christianity or other religions. Some Hindu language has become part of the American religious landscape, including words like mantra, which refers to a theme or focus believed useful in meditation. Ask your child if they have ever heard about anyone Hindu or about Hindu ideas, e.g., Gandhi.

What Is Islam?

Because of the continuing fascination with Middle Eastern countries and their continual presence in international news, an older child probably has heard of Islam and about its widespread popularity. But your child may learn more about Islam in its political application or misapplication than about its basic religious teachings. You can utilize your child's recognition of Islam and Moslems to initiate discussion; then help your child appreciate the complexities of Islamic belief and practice.

Islam was founded well after Christianity, in A.D. 622, in Medina, on the Arabian peninsula, by Mohammed the Prophet. Its sacred book is the Koran, which can be translated as "The words of God." You can suggest to your child that this book serves as the Moslem Bible.

Like its predecessors, Judaism and Christianity, which were begun nearby, Islam is a strictly monotheistic religion. It recognizes only one God and that Deity is called Allah. That is the origin of the familiar Moslem greeting, "Allah be praised." The Moslems, or followers of Islam, believe that Allah is all-powerful, all-fair, and all-merciful.

According to Islam, mankind is believed to be Allah's highest creation, but people are flawed and readily misled by Satan, an evil spirit. In the Koran, Allah is thought to have revealed to man all truth and the secrets of salvation. Moslems believe that Allah wants people to find the truth. Those who turn away from Satan and repent will return to a state of sinlessness, Paradise—a state of physical and spiritual enjoyment—with Allah.

These tasks are required of Moslem adults and children: (1) professing the faith, i.e., proclaiming "Allah is the only God," (2) praying five times per day; (3) offering goods for charity; (4) fasting on a designated Holy Day; and (5) making at least one pilgrimage to Mecca, the Moslem Holy City in Saudi Arabia. Your child may wish to compare and contrast these obligations with those of your religion. "Is that anything like the requirements of our religion?" "What do you think about these duties?"

When speaking to youngsters who are especially curious, or to older children about Islam, you may wish to distinguish between the two largest Moselm sects: the Sunni and the Shi'ah. A major difference between the two sects concerns the authority of Allah. While the Sunni believe that Allah predestines the fate of people, the Shi'ah stress that people can choose their own destinies by averting negative influences. Ask your child what he or she thinks of free will by saying, "Do you think you can have a big say in what happens to you, or do you think that is up to God?" You will learn a great deal about your child's approach to life through his or her reactions.

What Is Buddhism?

If you wish to discuss a religion very different from most Western religions, then you should consider Buddhist philosophy. Buddhism appears very exotic and foreign to Western ears at first, both because it is not God-focused and it's not as clearly optimistic about mankind's situation.

Also founded in India, Buddhism was begun about 525

B.C. by Gautama Siddhartha, the Buddha. The Buddha was said to have achieved enlightenment through intense solitude and meditation, and this became the central driving force for the religion. The primary text is called Tripitaka, a collection of the Buddha's teachings. Other basic elements of Buddhist philosophy and interpretation are revealed in a book called the Sutras.

You can emphasize to your child that Buddhism differs dramatically from religions most of us are familiar with. Without being too dramatic, tell your child that a Buddhist has a somewhat bleak picture of life. Buddhism asserts that the world is full of hardship and suffering, and that there is no ultimate overseer guiding destiny. The cycle of birth and rebirth observed by Hindus is also acknowledged in Buddhism. The Buddhist believes that the painful cycle continues because of wrong human desires and false worldly attachments—relations to both people and things.

The Buddhist does not look to a Deity for help or inspiration. Buddhism teaches that correct meditation will end the cycle and the suspended state of hardship. Meditative experiences may range from quiet contemplation to elaborate chants and temple rites, depending on sect customs and individual preferences. The supreme goal for the Buddhist is to reach Nirvana, a desirable state of void or nothingness. Buddhism teaches about this goal in the way that many religions in Western cultures speak about heaven or peace.

In the United States, Buddhist ideas often exist as an alternative to conventional religious ideologies. One form of Buddhism, Zen, which offers practical meditative techniques, has assimilated into popular culture and has been adopted by many people.

When considering Buddhism, think about whether there's an implicit view of a God. Make certain to assess your child's reactions to the suffering theme. Also, the idea of nothingness may be frightening and incomprehensible to children, so tread carefully with your child.

What Is Eastern (Greek) Orthodox?

Though the roots of the Eastern Orthodox Church are the same as other Christian religions, many children are unaware of the relationship. Children who are earnest calendar watchers, with a particular interest in holidays, may first notice this religion when they see a second Christmas (January 7) marked on the kitchen calendar and ask, "Why do these people celebrate Christmas at a different time?" You can respond by telling your child that the Eastern Orthodox religion functions on a different annual calendar (New Year's is January 14), but you can also take the opportunity to discuss this religion.

According to followers of this religion, which is sometimes called Greek Orthodox because of its geographic origins, the religion was founded in the year of the death of Jesus Christ—A.D. 33. *Orthodox* is a Greek word which literally means "true belief." The religion was inspired by the travels and teachings of four apostles of Jesus: Andrew (Constantinople or Istanbul); Mark (Alexandria); Peter (Antioch), and James (Jerusalem). The Eastern Orthodox Church was originally the same as the Catholic Church, but the two were divided over one thousand years ago. Followers do not look to a pope for guidance, but turn to a council of bishops called a synod.

The Eastern Orthodox Church emphasizes the Resurrection of Christ more than the Crucifixion. It sees God as one Being as well as a Trinity. It sees Jesus as truly a man in every respect but sin, and does not accept the notion of Immaculate Conception in conjunction with the birth of Mary. Also, it doesn't recognize a purgatory or transitional afterlife, nor does it allow divorce, except under special circumstances. Its bishops are the only ones required to abstain from marriage and sex.

Here again, you can ask your son or daughter: "How is this religion different from other Christian religions?" "Why do you suppose the people had a disagreement a thousand years ago?" "Is there anyone at your school who goes to a Greek Orthodox Church?"

Your child may also want to learn about some American-based minority religions. He or she also may wonder if all religions are ancient and started in faraway places. So I have selected two more recent additions to the world's religions. Depending on your region of the country, your child may well hear about the Mormon Church (The Church of Jesus Christ of Latter-day Saints), most of whose members live in the West, and the Quaker Society in the Middle Atlantic states. Here are a few basic ideas you can communicate about each.

What Is a Mormon?

The Mormon religion is a decidedly Christian belief system which accepts the teachings of Jesus Christ without exception. The Mormon people do not consider themselves Protestants or Catholics, however, but an independent Christian religion. The church emerged out of the inspiration of Joseph Smith in 1830. Smith was from New York

State and traversed the country to disseminate his ideas, only to be martyred in the process. The next church leader was Brigham Young, after whom Utah's Brigham Young University is named.

Mormons believe that the gospel of Christ was proclaimed by God before the world was created, and that it was known to the first man. They argue that mankind departed from God at the time of the great flood, and that people must restore the faith through teaching and hard work. They believe in a trinity of three distinct personalities and recognize the Virgin Birth of Christ. They maintain that God has always revealed His divinity to the whole world, not just to Israel or in ancient times. The revelation of God allows people to realize that God is actually a real Being.

The Mormon religion stresses education and missionary duty for each member, and they do not practice polygamy, as is sometimes rumored. In contrast to Catholicism, Mormons do not baptize infants but only those who can choose for themselves—considered by most to be children who are eight years old or older. There are no professional clergy in the Mormon Church, no priests or ministers, so it is everyone's responsibility to spread the faith. Mormons also believe in the sanctity of the family. They encourage members to have children early in life, and urge them to have several children.

It may be interesting to ask your child what he or she thinks about the idea of having many children. "Should this be a religious notion?" you can ask. Also, find out what your child has heard about the Mormon Church or about Brigham Young University. What were your youngster's expectations about the Mormon religion prior to your talk?

Discuss how the Mormon concept of God is very different from Protestant and Catholic images.

What Is a Quaker?

Another Western religion that your child may hear about as part of American history or in its contemporary practice is Quakerism, practiced by The Religious Society of Friends. Followers of this religion are commonly called Quakers. The religion was actually founded in England in the seventeenth century by George Fox, but it came to America with greater popularity during the eighteenth century and was well received in Pennsylvania and the surrounding area.

Quakers believe that God can be reached directly by the individual, and that no priest or preacher is required. A person can locate God through a search for "inward light"—an inner realization of Divine presence. Inward light is equated with the still, small inner voice in everyone, perhaps something like what your child may experience if he or she prays before going to bed. In this way, God is believed to speak in the present and God's vision is continuously revealed.

Like Mormons, Quakers consider themselves as distinct from the Protestant and Catholic Churches. Nevertheless, some Protestants and Catholics accept certain Quaker beliefs and even attend Quaker gatherings. Quakers emphasize absolute sincerity and tolerance among community members, and they seem to attract a broad following from diverse backgrounds as a result.

The focus of Quaker life is spirited fellowship among its members and group worship. Quaker religious services, called meetings, are not highly structured or intricately pre-arranged events. They occur without an ordained minister and they transpire without elaborate ceremony or ritual. Silence is central to the religious process at a Quaker meeting. In the absence of a formal written creed, the individual is compelled to arrive at his or her own system of belief. The individual spends most of the meeting attempting to allow the spirit of God to make itself known. It is through this method, the Quakers believe, that God claims His dominion over the entire world.

Of particular interest is the Quaker substitute for religious dogma, called Queries. These are sets of common questions put forth to guide a person along the path of faith. Typical Queries at a meeting include: "Are love and the unity of mankind among you?" "What are you doing to develop the conditions of peace?" "What are you doing to prevent the conditions of war?"

Concerning these Queries, why not ask your child what he or she thinks of this as a spiritual guide. You might ask your child if there are any such questions that he or she would like to ask.

What Is an Agnostic?

I would strongly urge you to find an opportunity to talk to your child about people who are doubtful about God. Speaking about people who doubt in a religious sense can be enormously helpful in understanding the experience of religious skepticism, whether it occurs in a believer or not. Agnosticism is not really a religion per se, but a perspective on life that significant numbers of people have in common.

We can think of agnosticism as a collective kind of skepticism.

Tell your youngster that an agnostic is not an atheist, since an atheist has eliminated the possibility of God but an agnostic has not. On the other hand, an agnostic is someone who suspends judgment about God. He believes that there are not sufficient grounds either for belief in God or refutation of belief. In explaining this to your child, try an analogy. For example, an agnostic is to God as an explorer is to a treasure that he has heard about but is not sure he believes is real.

For many agnostics, the existence of God is viewed as unlikely. An agnostic person does not accept any supernatural authority and usually maintains that a person should answer questions for himself or herself. An agnostic person is uncertain about good and evil, and does not accept the Bible as divinely inspired—though he recognizes the Bible's wisdom and guidance. As with the notion of God, the agnostic does not assume a stance when it comes to questions of afterlife. "There is no way to know about a heaven," the agnostic surmises, "without any evidence or sign."

It may help to furnish your child with an example of a person who practices agnosticism. The best example, of course, would be someone both you and your child know well. With that person's permission, talk about him or her to your child, and suggest to your child that he or she ask a few nonintrusive questions about the person's beliefs. As with many topics concerning God's existence, there is no substitute for direct learning through experience.

Warren, age twenty-seven, professes to be an agnostic. According to Warren, "I was brought up without any major religious push. I'm kind of a humanist, I guess. I believe in our ability to make things happen and improve the world. I believe we only have one life—it's kind of an accident of fate—so I want to make the most of it. I have a two-year-old. When he gets older, I'm going to tell him not to rely on the existence of a God. 'Take charge, yourself,' I'll say. 'There may not be a God.' "

Whether or not your child talks about or talks to a specific person, I would suggest that you ask your child: "Do you ever have doubts about God?" "Do you think it's all right if people doubt?" "What do you think of people who doubt?"

Exploring Religions Further

It's very important that your child follow up discussion of any of these religious systems with further investigation. That's really the only way your child can appraise religions and understand people of different religions.

For further information, you can write to the local or national offices of these religions. Or you can find more information at your local library or through your state's Council of Churches.

Encourage your child to read further about subjects of great interest. He or she can begin with an encyclopedia and then proceed to more specific books about religions, which should help to enliven his or her understanding. Also, suggest that your child ask other children at school about their religious backgrounds. Your child may find an eager spokesperson or two right in your neighborhood.

8

Discussing Your Religion: Judaism, Catholicism, Protestantism, Unaffiliated Belief in God

"Dear God,
    I am Lutheran and two of my best friends are Jewish. One other is different all together. He is from India.
    I think that it is not right that you left them out of Christmas. Please put them back in. They are very kind to me.

Love Always,
Ann
(age 9)"
FROM *DEAR GOD*

While some parents find it quite natural to stress the religion of their ancestry, these same parents are sometimes hard-pressed to explain the "why" behind their religious beliefs. Because certain beliefs have been maintained for centuries, it is easy to lose touch with the origins of religious experience. It is vitally important that a parent understand the bases of his or her religious beliefs and be able to express them plainly and openly to a child. While children may grow confused or rebellious when religion is inadequately explained, they are likely to grow up curious and respectful if a parent's beliefs are thoughtfully articulated.

"My family has always been Protestant through and through," says thirty-nine-year-old Kate, a mother of three. "But as to what that means exactly, other than going to church and working hard, no one really talked about it. When it came to raising my three children, I had to go back and do a lot of reading and thinking. And I had to ask myself, 'What do I believe Protestants stand for?' "

There are many Jewish, Catholic, and Protestant people like Kate, who have been raised with one of these religions but have not had the opportunity to examine fundamental beliefs. As a result, their ideas about religion are hazy and their ability to discuss the subject is limited. If you haven't been fortunate enough to receive a solid grounding in your heritage, then perhaps this is an excellent time to do so. If you have considerable background concerning your religion, then a refresher about basic tenets may be all that's required before you speak with your child.

When speaking about your religion of origin, remember to distinguish between institutionalized beliefs and your own personal preferences. For example, your religion may advocate fasting on a given day. You may choose to fast on that day. Or you may choose to abstain from the practice while still concurring in spirit with the rationale behind the fasting—appreciation for the gift of food. Be clear with your child on such issues. Explain why you practice or don't practice specific religious customs. Explain how your personal ideas of religion fit with formal religious tradition, if in fact they do. But also point out how your personal credo is unique and different. That is the best way I know to teach a healthy respect for religious individualism, along with community worship. Using the example of fasting, you might say that you believe in this practice because it helps you appreciate your everyday blessings of food.

As a way of contributing to your religious reflections, I have put together a summary of the three major religious traditions in American life. Use these descriptions as a convenient guide rather than as an extensive portrayal of great traditions—the religions are too rich and complex for that. But the summaries should help you consider the highlights of your religion and other traditions with your child.

Talking About Judaism

What Is Judaism?

If you're Jewish, or even if you are not, and your child asks about what it means to be a Jew, what would you say? Would you stress history or contemporary changes? Would you emphasize culture or religion? In asking these questions of parents, I've heard a great variety of responses. The following two illustrations provide an indication of how everyone's interpretation of a religion can be quite different.

"Judaism is what makes us Jews," thirty-year-old

Rhonda tells her five-year-old daughter. "We believe in one God who selected us to be His people. Our forefathers suffered but kept their faith in God. It is a miracle that the Jewish people have survived for five thousand years. It could have only happened because we believe in God."

Forty-one-year-old Janice, a mother of four, presents a somewhat different perspective on Jewry. "Jews are a group of people that we are a part of," Janice tells her children. "We have to do everything we can to keep the group going, because it almost ended with the Holocaust. For some people, being Jewish has a lot to do with holidays and rituals. But your father and I feel that our own culture is what is most important. For us, as we hope you will feel, being Jewish means identifying with the state of Israel. It's our obligation to make sure it remains the Jewish homeland," Janice concludes.

There are many other approaches and points of view that parents assume with children. However, there are a few generalities about Judaism that many parents will want to bear in mind. These general considerations account for both biblical and modern Judaism, and Jewry as both a religious and a cultural phenomenon.

You can tell your child that Judaism was the first religion to believe in a single God. This Deity is portrayed in the Old Testament of the Holy Bible, in conjunction with the patriarchs of the religion. Judaism reveals a lineage of colorful leaders who were purported to be chosen by God. These major figures include: Abraham, Isaac, Jacob, Joseph, Moses, and David. Jesus Christ was also part of this lineage, and he was the inspiration for the Christian religions of the world. He is not recognized by the Jewish religion as a significant figure in God's plan, however, nor is he viewed as divine.

To describe the basic tenets of Judaism to your child, emphasize that Jews believe in an omnipotent and just God. The God depicted in biblical stories is above all a God of justice. Jews believe that God chose the Jewish people to represent God's wishes on earth. Judaism holds that mankind's responsibility is to live in accordance with God's laws. The proper way to worship God, Judaism suggests, is to try to emulate those qualities which Jews perceive in God. Thus, since God is merciful, people should develop their ability to be compassionate. People should practice mercy with other human beings.

How can you sum up the primary tasks of a Jewish person, when Judaism contains so many specific laws and restrictions? You can focus on three fundamental demands of being a Jew. These are basic parts of the Sabbath service: (1) worship God as the one and only Deity ("Hear O Israel, the Lord is our God, the Lord is One"); (2) love learning and love to study The Five Books of Moses in particular; (3) do good deeds (*mitzvot*) and give charity (*tzedakah*). These things are required for claiming Judaism as a way of life.

Your child may be curious about the social aspects of Judaism, and indeed, owing to the directive concerning good deeds, civic obligation is stressed. Judaism explicitly urges people to be concerned about the welfare of others. Each person is believed to be linked with each other person and God is thought to be the origin of all such relationships. Thus, Jews are taught to be sensitive to their neighbors at an early age—a lesson that has helped the religion and the culture survive many perilous circumstances.

While God is thought to intervene in human affairs,

just as God did when the Red Sea was parted in the time of Moses, Jews do not believe God appears in the flesh. Unlike Christians, Jews do not believe in the incarnation of God, but instead envision God as a purely spiritual Being. Nonetheless, the spirit of God is believed to communicate directly with human beings rather than through an intermediary. No priest or leader is required for communication and prayer, as each Jew must make his or her own covenant with God just as Abraham and Moses did in ancient times.

"Why do some Jews observe all kinds of special practices and others do not?" your child may wonder. In response, you can say that modern Jews divide themselves into three groups depending on how they interpret Jewish law. Orthodox Jews accept the Bible literally, as some Protestants and Catholics do. Orthodox Jews believe the Bible is unalterable and mankind must devote the lifetime that God provides for obedience to God's wishes. The Orthodox life-style is a highly structured, ascetic way of living. There is considerable separation between men and women and households are run in a highly organized and solemn manner. Orthodox Jews use only Hebrew in their religious services, which run appreciably longer than the services of the other Jewish groups. Above all, Orthodox Judaism emphasizes a strict and absolute observance of the Sabbath (Saturday), and the unqualified observance of kosher dietary laws. That means partaking only of certain foods and specially prepared meats, not mixing meat and dairy products, and refraining from certain foods altogether (e.g., pork, shellfish).

Conservative and Reform Jews are much more relaxed in their understanding of Jewish laws and traditions. Conservative Judaism accepts much of traditional Judaism but sees the religion as evolving and continuously growing. Conservatives use a good deal of English along with Hebrew in their religious services and allow women a more prominent role in religious proceedings. They follow some Sabbath restrictions but frequently depart from others for the purpose of modernization (e.g., driving a car on the Sabbath).

Reform Judaism represents a more radical departure from traditional beliefs and practices. Reform Jews accept only the moral and ethical laws of the Bible as binding. As such, Reform Jews dispense with many traditional notions about the Sabbath and religious holidays. They stress rationality and intellectual understanding, rather than intense devotion or ritualistic deeds. In recent years, there has been a considerable push toward equality of the sexes among Reform Jews and this trend is also affecting the other groups. In a move that brings modern Jewry closer to modern Christian practices in style and ceremony, Reform services now include choirs and instrumental music.

If your child asks about religious services and Jewish holidays, what would you stress? You can point out a number of key terms and remembrances. Each of these Jewish groups meet in a synagogue or temple, where a rabbi ("teacher") oversees religious practice. The Sabbath service is led by a cantor who sings hymns and prayers. The focus of most services is The Five Books of Moses (*Torah*), along with generous portions of *Talmud*, sixty-three books of legal, ethical and philosphical writing. Other religious hymns and prayers, a good number written by King David of biblical importance, round out the service.

Among Jewish holidays, the Day of Atonement (Yom Kippur) and the Jewish New Year (Rosh Hashanah) in the fall and Passover (Pesach) in the spring are among the most important. Remember to tell your child the purposes of each event as well as the major symbols and rituals. Remember to ask which of these practices most appeal to your child, as well as which appeals the least.

Yom Kippur is the day that Jews repent for their sins and ask for God's forgiveness. This holiday seems a direct result of the Old Testament view of God as a judge and symbol of justice. Traditionally, Jews fast on this day in order to demonstrate their faith and focus on spiritual matters. Rosh Hashanah precedes Yom Kippur by a week and signifies the beginning of the Jewish calendar. It also marks the starting point for reflection and the purging of guilt, symbolically enacted by the tossing of bread crumbs into a brook or stream. Passover commemorates the great exodus of the Jews from Egypt through God's intervention. In thankful remembrance, Jews eat only unleavened bread and carefully prepared Passover food. At the ritual dinner called seder, Jews eat certain foods in a specific order and read out loud the story of the enslaved Jews' exodus from Egypt.

The family has long since been the center of Jewish life. With the ever-increasing mobility of Jews in America, families are much more separate than in any time in recent history. Jewish families now use religious holidays as a time to gather together.

There is a great deal of controversy about interfaith marriage in the Jewish community. Many Jews are adamantly opposed to an interfaith union because they fear that the Jewish people will disappear. Jewish law declares that a child is considered Jewish only if he or she is born of a Jewish mother. Nevertheless, the number of interfaith marriages continues to be high.

Suggestions for Jewish Parents

Depending on what being Jewish means to you, your guidance to your child can be as specific as you prefer. Ultimately, what you'll probably do is assess your child's needs and determine how Jewishness fits into that picture. I want to supplement your ideas with a few suggestions that have occurred to me in speaking with Jewish parents.

First and foremost, I would recommend that you stress the rich historical legacy of the Jewish religion. A five-thousand-year-old civilization is certainly worthy of recognition and your child should be as aware as anyone of Jewish lineage. With very young children, you can teach about historical figures through playing "a mix and match" game. Prepare for your child a list of major figures, including both men and women, and a second list of reasons for their importance. Mix up the items of each list and ask your child to match people with events. For example, "Solomon" might correspond to "known for his wisdom," or for "building a temple." "Joseph" might go with "the coat of many colors" or "interpreter of dreams." "Sarah" might be correctly matched with "mother of Isaac." The game should be fun and should not be treated as a scholastic test or exercise.

When it comes to discussion, try to relate each of these figures to the perpetuation of the Jewish religion. What role did each play? Perhaps more importantly, what does their contribution have to teach your child about life today? Whenever you are speaking about the Jewish legacy, remember to point out the willpower, strength, and sense of conviction that many leaders have called upon. Don't be afraid to show your child a sense of pride, if that is what you feel. Pride is a wonderful teacher and it can be contagious.

I would also suggest discussing biblical figures in real, nonfantastic terms. Point out to your child that these were human beings, with strengths and weaknesses, who played major roles in the history of the Jewish religion. Encourage your child to consider the motives of Joseph's brothers or the ambitions of Saul; inspire your child to imagine the predicaments of Job or the courage of the Maccabees. Try to help your child envision the actual human experience of these ancient heroes. This technique should help your youngster relate to historical figures as people. It should also focus attention on the universal qualities illustrated by the characters, beyond the battle scenes and the miraculous events. You can ask your child, "Do you see examples of these qualities in modern times?" "How about in people we know?"

Concerning Jewish holidays and rituals, I believe the clearest priority is to be explicit about the reasons behind related activities. Your child needs to know why you perform each and every task, not just how to perform those tasks. Be ready to say why you believe in the importance of a ritual, too. For example, if you do not eat bread on Passover, tell your child about the historical significance of that practice. But why does your family continue to abstain from bread? Is it because you identify with the suffering the Jews experienced in the land of Egypt? Or is it that you perpetuate Jewish culture by maintaining selected rituals? Why do you perform some rituals but not others? Be assured that your son or daughter will want to know, so be prepared.

Daniel, a thirty-year-old father of a newborn, expresses this regret. "My parents never told me why we did things—why we lit candles, why we fasted, why we ate matzoh. I always had to read about it," Daniel continued, "and I resented it. When my daughter is old enough, I'm not going to make that mistake. I'm going to explain things, even if it's 'a pain.' "

A good time to discuss rituals is prior to, during, or just after their performance. That way the event will be fresh in your child's mind. If your child does not ask about the basis of a religious practice, you bring it up: "Did you wonder why we celebrate _____ each year?"

While Judaism is an influential religion, Jews are relatively few in number and occupy a minority status in American life. It is important that your child not develop an adversarial relationship to other larger religions, as a way to protect his or her own faith or as a response to prejudice. Be certain not to propagate an "us vs. them" philosophy when it comes to comparative religions, for that will not serve your child well. You can guard against this by stressing the fact that Judaism is the forefather of the monotheistic religions of the world. At the same time, you can direct your child to consider the close historical kinship between Judaism and Christianity. Respect for other religions can only increase your child's pride in your religion and make your child a better person. So convey to your son or daughter that because the Jewish religion was the basis of a number of great religions, your roots are really the same roots that many other people have. And God is the source of everyone's life.

The Holocaust is a delicate subject that many Jewish parents must grapple with, sometimes in an effort to explain the experiences of deceased or psychologically wounded relatives. "What happened to my great-grand-mother?" your child may want to know. It is important that parents of all religions discuss the meaning of the Holocaust with their children, but only when their children seem emotionally ready. The Holocaust is a shocking and grotesque event, a twentieth-century nightmare which cannot be put to rest, but which must be broached with great care.

If your child hasn't heard about the Holocaust through school or television, it is very likely that he or she will sooner or later. Your child may already be curious about what the Holocaust was and why it happened. The Holocaust is the pivotal historical event for modern Jewry and perhaps the most profound spiritual challenge as well. Questions about God follow naturally from something as hard to discuss as the Holocaust. It even causes some adults and children to wonder if God exists, for how could God allow such suffering? For Jews, the Holocaust and the threat of extinction have prompted a tremendous, passionate interest in the state of Israel. For Christians, the Holocaust can also be seen as a modern crucifixion that must be considered on a theological level as well as a historical catastrophe.

"Why did those six million people die?" your child may wonder. It is important that you know some basic facts about the Holocaust, either through talking to survivors or reading the accounts of Holocaust writers like Elie Wiesel, Abba Eban, or Lucy Dawidowicz. If your child asks you this question, try to speak from the heart. If you feel that you don't have an answer, then say so—but also tell your child the possibilities that you have considered. Do you think that there is meaning in suffering? Do you believe that God cannot control everything on earth? Questions about the Holocaust are always elemental and answers always seem to be without closure. But all that anyone can ask of you as a parent is to respond to your child with faith and reason.

If it is hard for adults to comprehend the sheer ugliness of the Holocaust, it is nearly impossible for children to make any sense of it. As a Jewish parent, you will not want to downplay its impact, but you must not present the Holocaust as the only theme of modern Jewish life. Try to place it in a historical context. How has being a Jew changed because the Holocaust happened? Tell your child some details about the Holocaust but don't inundate him or her with horror and anguish. Temper your interest with protectiveness. Talk to your child about questions of faith that still trouble you when you think about the Holocaust. And speak to your child about the future too, for that also holds important questions about faith and God.

In considering what Judaism means, below are a number of intriguing questions which may be of special interest to children. Please use this as a stimulus for your own questions, which can be personally shaped to accommodate the personality and age of your child. Find out why your child believes his or her answers are true.

QUESTIONS FOR JEWISH FAMILIES

1. What does "chosen" mean?
2. Do you believe that Adam and Eve existed? Do you believe there was a Great Flood?
3. Why have school and knowledge been emphasized in the Jewish religion?
4. Are there psychological qualities that the Jewish people you know have in common? Why or why not?

5. Has the Jewish concept of God been predominantly a male concept?
6. Should men and women, boys and girls, sit together in the synagogue?
7. What do you think God feels about Christian people?
8. Do you wish that Judaism had a central figure like the pope in Catholicism?
9. What is your favorite holiday? Why?
10. What is your least favorite holiday? Why?
11. Do you have a favorite prayer?
12. Is there anything about the traditional Jewish picture of God that bothers you?
13. Should children be able to choose their own religion or group within a religion?
14. What does bar (bat) mitzvah mean?
15. Should there be more women rabbis?
16. When do you think the Messiah will come?
17. What is your opinion of Jesus Christ and his role in history?
18. Have you ever experienced anti-Semitism? How did you deal with it?
19. Where was God during the Holocaust? Why didn't He stop the horrible things that happened?
20. Is God too judgmental in the Old Testament?
21. How do you feel at Christmas and at Easter?
22. Should children fast on Yom Kippur?
23. What is the best way to communicate with God?

Talking About Catholicism

What Does It Mean to Be a Catholic?

Catholicism is so much a part of religious life in Western culture, both in fact and in fiction, that many people feel they know what a Catholic is without looking deeply into the religion itself. But Catholicism is, in fact, a very complex religion. Even if you are a devout Catholic, don't assume that your youngster understands Catholic beliefs and rituals. Take the time to discuss even highly popularized symbols of Catholicism, particularly because your interpretation of what a Catholic is may differ sharply from popular depictions.

Begin with fundamental details about the origins of Catholicism. Unfortunately, some children grow up with an appreciation for Christmas trees and Easter eggs but are not adequately informed about the significance of New Testament events. The accoutrements of religious holidays can captivate a child's interest, but spiritual explanations of life and of God's design can provide a lasting sense of fulfillment.

"I tried to give my kids Jesus," fifty-year-old Theresa says. "I tried to feed them Jesus's teachings and his parables," Theresa continued only half in jest. "What I mean to say is, a child has to have God in them from the time they are young. That's the only way to be sure they'll do right in the world."

When you sit down with your child, you can distinguish Catholicism from many later Christian religions by emphasizing that it was founded in the time of Jesus Christ. Explain that it is based on Christ's teachings, as communicated through his disciples and written in the Gospels.

The notion of the Holy Trinity is central to Catholic beliefs. However, because of its inherent complexity, it's one of the most difficult aspects of the faith for children to grasp. Catholic children that I have interviewed show surprising confusion about the Trinity, variously referring to it as "some part of the Mass," "a Catholic grammar school," and "like the three wise men." You may need to take a good deal of time in explaining the Trinity, but be patient with your child. Be sure to say that the idea is different from everyday life because God is something beyond reality. Be careful to point out that the Trinity represents three distinct images as well as one Being—God. Be mindful to suggest that the Holy Spirit represents an essence or a feeling, not a true ghost or demon.

Since much of your child's expectations about formal Catholicism may come from the Church, you should devote ongoing conversation to the Church's role—a role which is sometimes very controversial. "Who is the pope?" a six-year-old may ask. "Is the pope always right?" a ten-year-old youngster may wish to know. If you abide by some or all papal decisions, it is crucial that you clearly delineate the doctrine of papal infallibility. You can suggest to your child that the doctrine does not mean that the pope is always right in all aspects of his life. It does mean, however, that Catholics believe the pope to be designated by God to keep Catholics aligned with God. Catholics maintain that the papal position, not the man himself, is divinely guided.

In keeping with this philosophy, Catholics believe that the Church is the anointed supervisor of the Bible. Thus, the Church has the ultimate word on what is intended by a given passage. Your child may wonder if this is fair or not, so it will be up to you to express your opinion on the Church's authority. The more lucid and the more specific you can be, the more you will encourage your child to carefully think about the Catholic Church and its role in your child's young life.

"What's Mass for?" your child may question. Remember that Mass is a cornerstone to a Catholic's practice and worship. If you attend church regularly, the Mass will be familiar and distinct for your child—at least in regard to procedures. But how clear is your child, and indeed, how informed are you concerning the variety of symbolic meanings conveyed in the Catholic Mass? There are a number of meanings you can decipher for your child. You can relate that the Mass is a memorial for the death and resurrection of the Lord. You can note that the Mass is a sacrifice like the sacrifice that Jesus made when he died on the cross. You can also see the Mass as a sacred banquet in which church members receive the literal body and blood of Christ (Communion). Don't forget to ask your child: "Why else do we go to Mass?" and "What goes through your mind when you see people taking Communion?"

Children also are curious about and sometimes afraid of confession, the process in which Catholics reveal their sins and ask for God's forgiveness. What's the purpose of confession? your child may wonder. Does it work? he or she may secretly question. If you believe in confession, tell your child why you feel it is a fundamental part of the Catholic religious experience. You may wish to delineate the different types of sins that are recognized, as well as the types of penance your child can anticipate. In any case, it is vital that you explain to your child in calm but straightforward terms how confession may fit in with a person's healthy development.

There are a number of other major subjects you will probably wish to address, given the place of these topics in Catholic dogma. Purgatory is one such notion in the Catholic religion that some Catholics adhere to. Purgatory is the intermediary state in afterlife where souls must go if they are not ready for salvation but have not committed any serious sins. Some Catholics believe that purgatory will cease to exist after Christ's return and the last judgment is at hand. Because of its mysterious and psychologically emotive nature, purgatory is frequently a source of rich fantasy for children. "Are you just hanging onto a rope the whole time?" one youngster asked. Children imagine all sorts of colorful backgrounds and arrangements for purgatory. Ask your child directly, "What do you think purgatory would be like?"

The Catholic religion also recognizes the living presence of Satan, the Devil or Antichrist. Satan is the force that acts in concerted fashion to counter the will of God. Satan is a spirit of high intelligence and nonpareil evil. While not all temptations may be attributable to Satan, Satan's task is to torment and tempt people into sin. Sin is the method by which Satan achieves power over people. The Catholic religion, like many others, emphasizes the insidious and coercive manipulation that Satan is capable of. Owing to movie depictions, children have very vivid ideas about the Devil. If Satan is a word that your child recognizes, probe to see what your child's fantasy of Satan is. You can examine this by saying, "Do you know what Satan is?" "What do you think Satan is like?"

Catholics believe fervently in the spiritual meaning of marriage, and as such, many steadfastly oppose divorce under nearly all circumstances. You can explain to your child that God sees marriage as a sacred bond between two people. "Many people see that bond as unalterable," you can further clarify with your child, "one that should not be broken." I would suggest getting your child's view of marriage. "Do you think people should always stay married—no matter what?" you might offer. Or, concerning people of other religions, you may inquire, "Should Catholic people marry people of other religions if they love them?"

When you discuss the major holidays that Catholics celebrate, you will probably want to stress how these are traditional family events. The roles that Christmas and Easter have in your family life are no less important than their original theological significance. Talk to your child about what each of these holidays means to your family, how it changes family members and how it affects your life-style—not just in December or April but throughout the year. Ask your son or daughter, "Do you like the way we celebrate Christmas (or Easter)?" "What could be different?" It's also okay to let them know if you wish they acted differently on the holidays, or if there are some related feelings you've kept to yourself. The holidays are fine inspiration for family disclosure and honesty.

The Catholic Church is quite vocal about many social issues. Perhaps these topics will arise naturally in family discourse, especially with your older children. The Church has long been vehemently opposed to abortion and discourages Catholics from using artificial birth control methods, though many Catholics depart from its teaching on this subject.

The Church also demands that priests and nuns, religious persons who devote themselves unequivocally to God's service, be celibate and take a vow not to pursue worldly desires, such as money and expensive goods. The Church places great emphasis on modesty for the purpose of preventing sex from being overvalued or cheapened.

Suggestions for Catholic Parents

Through talks with Catholic children, I have found a few themes which come up again and again. Issues of papal authority, marriage, the Trinity, sexuality, the gender of God, and the Christmas spirit are evident in many Catholic children. To offer a few ideas and some support, I want to present some observations concerning Catholic child-rearing.

I think that it helps matters a great deal if a parent is candid about how they view the pope. Therefore, I would recommend being explicit about what you believe the pope's role to be. It is also important to acknowledge to your child that not every Catholic follows the Vatican in a diligent way. "Some people like to be independent," you might choose to say. In any case, how do you feel about the current pope? What qualities do you see in him? Say how you feel in an open-ended way, allowing room for a child's early impressions. Ask your son or daughter to say what the pope does. Unless it seems premature, see what your child thinks about the idea of a pope or about the current leader of the Church.

Every Catholic child is taught early on that marriage is sacred but some youngsters don't really know why. "Why is divorce bad?" a psychologically minded child may want to know. What would you say in response? Would you say divorce is immoral? Would you say it tears families apart? That it represents the breaking of a vow, or would you stress its symbolic meaning in the Catholic religion? Perhaps you are not at all certain that divorce is always wrong. Is it okay to depart from traditional Catholic teaching on this subject?

Bring up these questions for family discussion and have everyone contribute their opinions. Even young children can understand the notion of marriage, so the conversation should not exclude them.

"I believe in marriage as a sacred rite," forty-six-year-old Anthony comments. "I always have. You get only one choice so you should make it a good one. What do I tell my kids? I say you have to decide for yourselves. But I believe that you will be happy if you find a good person and try to make it work with them. I think a lot of people give up too easy. Marriage demands work. You gotta believe in it."

Whatever you say to your child about marriage and/or divorce, try to include a statement about God's role. What does God have to do with getting married or getting divorced, if anything? God's role in both is a critical element in Catholic doctrine.

If your child asks about the Holy Trinity, be especially clear about the relationship of God, the Father, and Jesus and the Holy Spirit. One popular example is to compare the Trinity to an egg. Just as the yolk, the white of the egg, and the shell are all parts of the same whole, the Holy Spirit, Jesus, and God, the Father, are all part of God. Because it utilizes a familiar household object, this illustration is particularly helpful with inquisitive youngsters.

The most pressing interest among Catholic children I have spoken with concerns Jesus. "How can Jesus be both the Son of God and also be God?" Is your child concerned or curious about this? Make sure that your child understands the basic tenet of the Trinity. For now, that's probably enough.

With so much attention being paid to the Church's views on sexual matters, it's advisable to tackle the tough subject of religion and sexuality. It is important that these topics aren't seen by your child as mutually exclusive. But what should a parent communicate about these matters? Let your child know why the Church is concerned about relevant social issues. But emphasize that both religion and sexuality are good things, and that people get into trouble when they misunderstand or deviate from a full appreciation of the world God has provided, which includes both of the above.

Ask your child about guilt too. "Do you ever feel guilty?" "What kinds of things do you do sometimes that make you feel bad?" Be aware of any unreasonable or obstructive guilt your child may be festering. Remember that religious belief is intended to allow people to live more complete lives, not inhibit people from natural expression.

You may also want to speak with your child about gender issues. "Do priests and nuns perform different functions in the Church?" your son or daughter may wonder. "Is God a He since Jesus was a man?" The male emphasis in the Catholic liturgy is now a common source of debate in lay and clerical circles. Discussion of gender themes in Catholicism belongs in your home too. Are there aspects of your church's service that you disagree with? Do you feel that the Mass speaks equally to men and to women? Tell your child what you think and ask your child to think about these issues during the next service you attend together. Invariably, you will need to address whether you like the Mass as it is or whether you would like to see changes made.

Finally, Christmas is so significant to Catholicism, and so appealing to children in particular, that it demands special attention. Set aside an evening or two in early December of each year to discuss the spirit of Christmas. Take some time and shut off the televisions and stereos. Ask family members to talk about what Christmas means. For one family member, Christmas might mean a time for bright lights and singing. For someone else, it might suggest a time of peace. Christmas can mean something unique to each member of your family. Of course, for everyone, it ultimately will mean the day of Christ's birth. Discuss with your child why this is significant to you.

This will probably proceed best if family members are spontaneous, honest, and open. If it's feasible, include grandparents as well. The important thing is that adults and children share in the social and introspective experience. The atmosphere to inspire is one of warmth, togetherness, and open-mindedness. This will help make Christmas an even more spiritual experience for your child than it might be otherwise.

Here is a list of questions which reflect a cross section of Catholic themes and issues for parents to ponder when talking to children.

QUESTIONS FOR CATHOLIC PARENTS

1. What is the role of forgiveness in the Catholic religion?
2. How does being a Catholic in America differ from being a Protestant in America?
3. What do you believe heaven is like? Who will go to heaven?
4. What contemporary Catholic person do you most admire (e.g., Mother Teresa, Pope John Paul II, etc.)? Why?
5. What is the role of family in the Catholic religion?
6. Is there more emphasis on the New Testament or Old Testament in your church or home?

7. What other religions do you admire?
8. What should children know about the pope?
9. Is confession relevant for children?
10. Should priests marry and have families of their own?
11. Should women be allowed to be priests?
12. What are your views about abortion? About the Church's position on abortion?
13. Are Catholic children brought up differently from other children? If so, how?
14. Is the Catholic concept of God a close image or a distant one?
15. How do Catholic grammar schools compare with public schools? Catholic high schools? Colleges?
16. What does the observance of Lent mean to you?
17. What would Jesus say about modern Catholicism?
18. What is Mary's role in the Catholic religion?
19. What is the significance of the rosary?
20. What does the notion of Resurrection mean for everyday life?
21. How are you bringing up your child differently from the way your parents raised you?
22. What qualities are necessary for good teaching in a Catholic school?
23. Does your child know about the less popularized holidays (e.g., Ascension Thursday, Ash Wednesday)?

Talking About Protestantism

What Does It Mean to Be a Protestant?

If you're Protestant you are probably well aware of a religious tradition that includes the earliest settlers of our country, and you may have passed that on to your child.

Awareness of Protestant history can help a child better understand the common qualities Protestant denominations share.

Perhaps with the aid of a story or picture book, explain to your child that Protestantism is the name for several religious groups which were formed during the Great Reformation of the early sixteenth century. The most significant action was a plea by theologian Martin Luther for greater religious freedom, as he posted his Ninety-five Theses in 1517. Luther's monumental defiance culminated a steady movement away from the authority of the pope in Rome. This led to Protestant religions that have formed, over the centuries, in accord with Luther's beliefs, in Europe and then later in America.

The original Reformation advocated a series of basic principles, tenets which many of the modern Protestant denominations continue to accept in one form or another. If your child asks you how Protestant groups are alike, you can explain that most Protestants believe that the Bible is the only reliable source of God's word. Protestants do not believe that a person hopes to go to heaven based on his or her actions alone. Instead, faith in God is also required for salvation. That view is best explained through an illustration. For example, while being kind and considerate makes a little boy a better person, the little boy needs to believe in God, too, in order to be a Christian. Try to think up an illustration that will have special meaning for your son or daughter.

Other Protestant beliefs should be equally emphasized. When you speak about the origins of the Protestant-Catholic schism, point out that the first Protestants did not reject all prior Christian traditions by any means. They just turned away from church authority, especially the pope. Thus, Protestants want people who teach about religion to teach only what God literally says—they are dubious about excessive interpretation. In other words, the Bible itself is what they use to base their beliefs on. Protestants have made many symbolic and ritualistic departures from the Catholic mass, which traditionally has been more formal.

It is important that you explain to your child that there are many Protestant denominations or groups which differ in subtle but important ways from each other. Your child will want to know how your denomination compares with those of his or her schoolmates. Below are brief descriptions of five Protestant groups which remain prominent: Lutherans, Methodists, Presbyterians, Baptists, and Episcopalians.

If you are **Lutheran,** your child should know that the Lutheran Church is named after Martin Luther and it began as a testament to him, shortly after the Reformation. Lutherans see Luther as a great teacher and liberator, but not as a saint or prophet. You will probably want to clarify that with your child.

Make sure to point out some of the distinguishing highlights of your faith. Note that in the spirit of religious liberalism, a Lutheran considers every Christian a saint as well as a sinner. That is an interesting notion, since it implies that people have both good and evil in them. Consider asking your child, "Can the same person do bad things as well as good things? Can you think of an example?" (e.g., stealing a toy from a schoolmate and also doing extra household chores voluntarily because Mom is sick).

You may also wish to discuss sin in greater detail, particularly with your older children. Observe that Lutherans believe sin to be a basic condition of life; people must learn to free themselves from sin. The goal of a Christian life, according to the Lutheran outlook, is complete obedience to God by obeying what the Bible says. The Lutheran view of God is ultimately a Being that grants forgiveness and salvation to human beings as a gift. So ask your child, "How do you think it is possible to get closer to God and obey God's will?"

If you are a **Methodist,** you'll want your son or daughter to appreciate that the Methodist religion reflects ideas which grew out of the Protestant Reformation and the teachings of Englishman John Wesley. Wesley preached in the early and middle eighteenth century. Stress that the love of God with the entire soul and mind is a Methodist teaching, an outgrowth of Wesley's philosophy.

To be a Methodist, a person must believe that Jesus Christ is God's son, part of the Trinity, and he must believe the New Testament. But a person must also believe that all truth is expressed in the words of Christ the Messiah and the Bible. A Methodist prioritizes faith in God over religious rules and rituals and believes in purity of thought as a way to approach God. A Methodist must also pledge allegiance to a social creed, a tenet which states that religion must be active in real-world, pragmatic reforms. That is a reflection of the social conscience, which Methodists believe is God's will.

In contrast to other Protestants, Methodists refer to three religious books. Your child should know that these books are the Bible, *The Book of Hymns,* and *The Book of Discipline. The Book of Hymns* was written by John Wesley and his brother, Charles. *The Book of Discipline* reveals a number of covenants which Methodists have agreed upon for common prayer and belief. With reference to these works, available at any Methodist church, you can discuss with your child how each contributes to your family and to the lives of other Methodists.

If you are **Presbyterian,** then your discussion with your child may be somewhat different. Inspired by English thinker John Calvin, Presbyterianism refers to a particular form of religious governing rather than a unique religious doctrine. The Presbyterian Church is governed by a group of leaders who represent the supreme authority on all procedural matters. As your child may know, there are teaching elders and ruling elders. Teaching elders are ordained ministers while ruling elders are members elected from church ranks, whose counsel is sought by the teaching elders on religious matters.

Like other Protestant denominations, Presbyterianism sees the Bible as the ultimate source of authority, guidance, and inspiration. Presbyterianism teaches that God employs chosen men to reveal divine intentions, but no man should intercede between God and the individual. In contrast to Catholics, Presbyterians offer their confessions directly to God rather than to a minister.

The Presbyterian religion has few symbols or ornate icons. In fact, most Presbyterian churches display only an empty cross. Presbyterians believe that Christ's Resurrection, not his Crucifixion, should be the center of mankind's attention. I would recommend that you mention this to your child and then inquire: "What do you think about when you see the cross in church?"

The **Baptist** religion also grew out of the Reformation and then later out of the Separatist and Puritan movements. As a result of these influences, Baptists have retained an independent and distinct character among Protestant denominations: In particular, Baptists have been noted for purity, responsibility, and tolerance of other religions in their worship.

Baptists believe that every church member is an evangelist; that means that every member is responsible for spreading Baptist ideas and the worship of God to others. Baptists also believe that every person must choose to be a Christian for himself or herself. Therefore, Baptist parents do not baptize their children at birth, for baptism must be a rite freely chosen by each boy and girl. Try to probe your child's view of baptism. Does your child understand how Baptist views and practices differ from some other Christians? Explain why you think free choice is important.

In keeping with their emphasis on individual decisions, Baptists stress the independence of local churches rather than the authority of a central church. They are strong advocates of religion as independent from state or political considerations. Theologically, Baptists, unlike many other Protestants, do not recognize divorce, except in cases of adultery. Interestingly, while Baptists have faith in a life after death, most do not readily accept the notion of a loving God who condemns some of His children to eternal hell. That topic is a natural one for family discussion if you feel your child won't be frightened by it. You can begin with a broad query like, "Where do you think people go after they die?"

Episcopalians are the Protestants who perhaps most resemble Catholics in their beliefs and practices. If you are Episcopalian, you can tell your child that the church is one of the self-governing organizations within the Anglican Communion of Churches, more commonly known as the

Church of England. Since the time of the English monarch Henry VIII, the Church of England has been the mother church for all Anglican churches.

Episcopalians see their bishops as their main spiritual figures and symbols of cohesion within the Church. While believing Protestant and Catholic ideals, Episcopalians reject the dominion of the pope but retain many traditional rituals. There is also some variation from Catholic practices. For instance, Episcopalians believe in confession but make that practice optional. Episcopalians do not demand that priests remain celibate. Suggest that your child speak with a Catholic friend and a Protestant friend of a different denomination, and see how being an Episcopalian compares and contrasts with these other neighboring religions.

You can also refer to *The Book of Common Prayer* along with the Bible as sources of information about worship. One emphasis which you may wish to pursue, which distinguishes the Episcopal religion from others, is the interaction of reason and Gospel teaching. Episcopalians attempt to look at life rationally and this influences their view of religious *dogma*. Thus, they see salvation as synonymous with religious health and wholeness of life. You may choose to speak with your child about how rational thought and faith can exist side by side, as so many Episcopalians believe.

Suggestions for Protestant Parents

Offering general suggestions for Protestant parents is a bit more difficult than for other parents, given the amount of diversity of Protestant denominations. But there are a few ideas that many Protestant parents may want to bear in mind.

The first thing that you should consider doing is distinguishing for your child the major differences among the Protestant denominations themselves. Some children are confused about what distinguishes a Methodist from a Lutheran, or what differentiates specific denominations. To avoid confusion, try to explain the basic differences to your child, or take him to the library and find religious books for children.

For youngsters who are old enough to comprehend categories, a simple chart of religions—like a spelling chart—may prove helpful. With a solid foundation in the different religions, your child will be able to follow world or local events that involve religious groups. Your child's awareness will be heightened in a variety of ways if he or she learns more about different religions.

Protestant families should also spend extra time discussing how Protestant religious themes have worked their way into American culture. Protestant children should be aware of the religious views of the Pilgrims and the founding fathers of our country. They should know, for example, that men like George Washington and James Madison were devout Episcopalians and that the Protestant work ethic is the belief that hard work reaps its own reward. These are clear examples of Protestant religious values that have been assimilated by the country in a secular way.

Because many Protestant groups are very education-oriented and even intellectual (e.g., Unitarians, Presbyterians), you may wish to balance this with discussion of religion as a visceral or emotional experience. Remember to keep in mind that Protestant religions focus on faith in

God alone, and faith is as much an emotional as an intellectual experience. You can say to your son or daughter, "For me the presence of God feels like . . ." And you follow that with the question, "When you think about God, what does that feel like to you?"

In my contact with Presbyterian children, I have detected a view of a God who is very concerned with the orderliness of the universe. Protestant children often talk about religion in terms of how it provides order and structure in people's lives. According to twelve-year-old Mark, a Baptist child, God provides order through "help in problem solving" and "making sure that things happen in a way that makes you learn from them." Ask your son or daughter, "How did God organize the world?" and "Is there a way you wish God would make things clearer or more orderly?"

You can also discuss how God affects the life of your child. Among other questions that you can consider are the following, compiled to address the needs of Protestant parents from a variety of denominations.

QUESTIONS FOR PROTESTANT PARENTS

1. How well does your church suit your family's needs? Does the church satisfy your need for religious direction, for community, and for a sense of God's presence?
2. In what ways do you feel largely similar to or different from Catholics?
3. Are your child's grandparents involved in the religious life of your family? If so, is this a help or a hindrance? How could their involvement be healthier?
4. Do you think people have free will? What does your

child think? Is free will good or bad? What implications does it have in one's life?

5. Have you attended many services of other Protestant denominations besides your own? How would you compare them?

6. What is distinctive about a Protestant Christmas? About Christmas in your denomination?

7. What secular American values are based in Protestant teaching?

8. Has public education gone too far away from formal religious influence, or even from informal religious consideration? Or is it a necessary safeguard?

9. Do you believe that a person must be a Christian in order to go to heaven? What does it mean to be a Christian?

10. How significant is God in your life? How significant do you want God to be in the life of your child?

11. Does your church treat men and women equally? How does this compare with sex roles in your family?

12. Are there any changes you would like to see in your religion when it comes to gender roles?

13. Do you believe that evil exists? How would you explain the concept of evil to your child?

14. Is it okay for adults to question God? Is it okay for children? Does your child know this?

15. How can you help your child learn more about his or her religious heritage?

16. How is being a Protestant today different from when your parents were your age? How do you imagine it will be different when your child is your age?

Talking About the Unaffiliated Belief in God

What Is an Unaffiliated Believer?

Some families and individuals march to the tune of a different spiritual drummer. While these individuals may have been raised in the major traditions just described, they have decided that formal religion is just not for them. Or alternatively, they have grown up in families which were unaffiliated to begin with. Nonetheless, these individuals come together as couples and continue to pursue an earnest, noninstitutionalized belief in God. If that description fits you and your spouse, then how have you decided to teach your child about God?

Many people who do not identify with formal religion do not wish to label their beliefs at all. Whatever you choose to consider yourself, you have probably declined formal religious teaching because you found it lacking or insufficient. You may have simply found that it did not convincingly address the questions that you have posed about life. Or you may feel that the experience of God must be direct and unmitigated; perhaps you see formal religion as an interference.

If that describes you, then you are not alone. While it is difficult to offer a precise figure, it is likely that millions of Americans may fall under this description. You can tell your children that. And you can explain that not joining a formal religion does not mean that you are not religious—it just means that you define belief in God a bit differently. You may also wish to distinguish between religious teachings and religion as an institution. Certainly, it is possible to feel reverence or awe or love of God and not be a member of a church or synagogue.

Do you emphasize human experience as a source of spiritual guidance rather than supernatural belief in the Bible? Then say that to your child and explain how your view departs from those of your friends and neighbors. Do you have a different view of famous religious figures like Moses or Jesus? Articulate for yourself and for your child what your view is. Are you more action-oriented than prayer-oriented? Then tell your child why you believe prayer is less important. Are you opposed to religious hierarchies and authority? Then delineate for your child how your opinion formed and what the dangers of such authority are. But don't just speak about what you are against. It is essential that your child also hear about what you do believe in, so that he or she has a coherent belief system to consider.

You may choose to focus your discussions on the notion of God itself. Please refer to the earlier chapter on images of God as a springboard for your thinking. How is your concept of God special and distinct from the God images of the major formal religions? How does it resemble those conceptions? If you can outline responses for your child in a systematic and compelling way, I believe your child will grow up with a coherent view even if your ideas are not bolstered by formal religious training. But it will be the strength, clarity, and courage of your convictions that determine your child's understanding of God, and his or her own spiritual development.

Suggestions for Unaffiliated Parents

I would strongly urge you to expose your children to the teachings of formal religions as well as to your own belief. Whatever your views of the world's many established religions, it is helpful and enriching for your child to learn about them. That is how your child will gain an appreciation for how different people have responded to the mystery of God.

You should also consider emphasizing freedom of choice in your child's decisions about God and about religion. You must ask yourself, "Do I feel it is acceptable for my child to choose a formal religion as a way to celebrate God?" Your answer to that question will determine in large part the kind of atmosphere you create in your home when it comes to religious belief.

"I try to take time with my sons and explain things carefully," says forty-five-year-old Bob, an unaffiliated father of two. "Since we're not members of a church, where else are our kids going to learn about ethics and morals but us? Sometimes I think because we spend a lot of time with them, they take religious ideas more seriously. My wife is particularly good with them—she talks to them more about God than I do."

Unaffiliated parents like Bob must assume great responsibility for their children's religious education. The potential benefits can be considerable since high parental involvement can often stir a child's interest. What is most important is that your child is not left in the dark about what you believe. In order to facilitate your talks, you might prepare a brief summary of your beliefs for the whole family to discuss. That may also be a help to parents who embrace more formal religions, too.

In addition to these subjects, unaffiliated parents should find the following questions helpful when talking to their children about God.

QUESTIONS FOR UNAFFILIATED PARENTS

1. Are you content with your life-style when it comes to religion? Is your child?
2. What are your most memorable experiences of God? Have you described them to your child?
3. What do you believe to be the major pitfalls of formal religion?
4. What is your view of Jesus Christ? Other Old and New Testament figures?
5. How much do you and your spouse agree or disagree when it comes to religion?
6. Do you think there is something to be gained by children from religious ritual?
7. Do you think God is unknowable?
8. Do you wish you could find a religious community you could feel comfortable with?
9. What are the religious backgrounds of your child's friends? Does he or she ever talk about this? What is said by your child and you?
10. How did you feel about your parents' religious views when you were growing up? How do you feel now?
11. How do you think your child feels about your views now? How do you think he or she will feel twenty years from now?
12. Are there religious figures, living or deceased, that you admire? Have you talked to your child about them?
13. If you celebrate Christmas, or some other conventional holiday, how do you think your celebration differs from your neighbors' who subscribe to a formal religion? What does your child think about the way you do or don't celebrate religious holidays?

14. How are your views alike or unlike an agnostic person's? An atheistic person's?

15. What are the most important guidelines of living? Have these changed in recent years?

16. What would you like your child to know that you find difficult to tell him or her about religion?

17. List the first five words that come to mind when you say: a. Protestant b. Catholic c. Jewish. Have your child perform the same exercise.

18. Do you believe in an afterlife? What have you communicated to your child about this? Were you influenced by the depictions of formal religious teaching?

19. Have you read the Bible or another major religious work? What were your impressions?

20. Do you believe in the notion of sin? Have you said anything to your child about what you believe?

21. Were religious beliefs a major consideration in your choice of spouse?

22. Who was most instrumental in the formation of your religious views?

23. Do you have friends or relatives who share your religious views? How often do you communicate with them about God? Do your children know each other well?

24. Have you ever been through a period of intense doubt? What was it like? What would you like to tell your child about that experience?

25. What would you say to your child if he or she said, "I don't believe in God"? Alternatively, what would you say if your child said, "I want to be a Christian," or "I want to be Jewish."

9

The Interfaith Family: A Special Phenomenon

"Dear God,
  My mom is Jewish and my dad is Catholic. My mom says this makes us even more special. Two is better than one.
  Do you like to mix things up like this?
  See you on all the holidays!

                    Love you,
                    Beth
                    (age 9)"
                    FROM *DEAR GOD*

Communicating with a child about your religion and background is seldom clear and uncomplicated, but sometimes it is especially challenging. This is often true for interfaith couples. They live in a world of difficult decisions, especially once children come along, and compromise about religion may be their way of life. This situation is increasingly common in America among Protestants, Catholics, Jews, and many others as more people choose marital partners without regard to religious background. Continuing increases in interfaith marriages could mean changes in the shape of religious worship as we know it, and will certainly have significant implications for the religious education of children.

Bringing up a child in an interfaith family is a special phenomenon worthy of careful consideration. The interfaith couple today is in a peculiar situation. Husband and wife frequently face moral dilemmas in speaking to their children about religion, but often have little formal religious or psychological guidelines to rely upon. While every interfaith family is unique, the basic challenge in most cases is similar: to bring together two diverse histories, to satisfactorily encourage a child to have faith, and to explore many possibilities of faith. In this chapter, we will outline some of the major issues for interfaith couples and offer a few suggestions for healthy religious guidance.

The most obvious concern for an interfaith couple is the separate set of perspectives they bring to family life. Coming from different religious backgrounds, husband and wife are faced with the formidable task of integrating those views into a coherent theological view in the home. For example, a Catholic parent is brought up to believe that baptism is necessary for salvation; a Jewish spouse may see baptism as a betrayal of his or her faith. When it comes to bringing up a child, the challenge is even more imposing. How can parents of different religious backgrounds teach their children about religious beliefs, practices, and the notion of God?

"The hardest thing," says thirty-one-year-old Audrey, a Protestant married to a Hindu, "is to explain together what you believe in and what we are worshipping. Coming from different religions can give you an unusual vantage point at times, but it's not always conducive to talking about

God. Since my husband was brought up with an Eastern way of looking at things, it may be a little more necessary for us to spell things out for our daughter about how we're similar," Audrey concludes.

As Audrey and other interfaith parents attest, the central issues for most couples of dissimilar religions are quickly apparent once children reach three or four years of age, if not much sooner. Couples must determine what religion or religious beliefs to offer to their children and what to tell their children about God. These are the core concerns which in large part will determine the shape and success of an interfaith family.

What Will Your Religion Be?

If you have an interfaith marriage, what religion should you offer to your child? You have several weighty choices, each with its own strengths and weaknesses.

You can choose one religion or the other, from the husband's or the wife's background, and make that the religion of your new family. For example, a committed Catholic father and a nominal Protestant mother might elect to bring up their child as a Catholic. The main advantage of this child-rearing strategy is that the child is raised in a single religious environment, as most youngsters are. Whether they are sent to religious school or not, children have a better chance to embrace religion if they concentrate on one coherent set of beliefs and practices. For the parent whose religion is not observed, the fundamental task is to keep an eye out for any possible resentment or guilt. Each parent must be entirely comfortable with the family's choice of religion.

The main disadvantage is that the socialization of children will be one-sided and fail to reflect the backgrounds and experiences of both parents. Also, this approach may alienate one side of the extended family. A child will still be curious about the neglected religion but will have no ready means to pursue that natural curiosity. A child may resent his or her parents for inhibiting such an important aspect of the family's heritage. This approach can be quite confusing to children unless both parents and their relatives are very clear and consistent.

Not knowing about her father's past was a prevailing concern for Karen, a young woman with whom I attended college. Karen was brought up to believe that she was Episcopalian, though her family never went to church or worshipped at home, and that both of her parents were Episcopalian by birth. Her family was not religious when Karen was a child, so she was reared with general Protestant values, but without a specific church affiliation. When Karen was twenty, she met and became engaged to a young Jewish man. After some consideration, she decided to convert to Judaism and began special classes to initiate the process. It was only then that Karen learned from her father that he was Jewish by birth. Karen was understandably upset and confused by this revelation. Prevented from learning of her father's past as a little girl, Karen was now pursuing that religion as a young adult. Had she known of her father's Jewish background, her decision to convert to Judaism might have been much easier.

An alternative to a single religious focus is to raise children in both parents' respective religions. Thus, a child of a Mormon father and a Catholic mother would learn about Mormonism and about Catholicism. This approach also has its benefits and its liabilities. The major benefits are: a child has the freedom to choose which religion he or she prefers; the family can celebrate more holidays and rituals, which can strengthen family bonds; the variety of ideas may inspire more vivid discussion about views of God; and a child exposed to such diversity may become more interested and open-minded about religion. These clear advantages need to be balanced in your decision by some equally salient liabilities, such as: the confusion a child may experience while learning the tenets of two religions when learning about one is hard enough; a family's sense of not belonging to any one community or group; an implicit feeling of guilt and upset in a child who feels that he or she must ultimately choose between the parents who represent the religions; the absence of a coherent religious dogma, replaced by opposing messages that are difficult to follow. Thus, the two-religion child may have a richer childhood experience, but such a youngster may suffer from lack of clarity and direction.

The issue of conflicting messages about religion is troublesome for many interfaith families, and as such, it demands extra special care and attention. For example, a Jewish-Christian couple might have to deal with their different views of Jesus Christ. Is it reasonable for people of these different backgrounds to reach a consensus? How will each speak about Jesus? Is he God or a man?

In few other situations is the possibility of confusing a child so evident. But the paramount importance of self-awareness for each parent is also quite clear. Each parent must know himself and what he believes about Jesus. The

Jewish parent may wish to consider any latent fear or prejudice about this topic. The Christian parent must be concerned with any prejudice on his or her part. Both must avoid any subtle attempts to persuade or proselytize. Whatever the individual preferences of the couple, a uniform decision of how to treat this subject is mandatory. You may not agree with each other on every religious issue, but you must concur when it comes to expressing this difference in front of your child.

You might tell your child that although your beliefs are different, you still love each other and, of course, your child. If God is love, then that will overcome things that confuse us or make us disagree. Your joint openness and respect for each other will undoubtedly serve as a great comfort to your child.

In contrast, some interfaith parents wish to avoid these embroiled difficulties. They may believe that the best thing to do is to bring up a child without the heavy blanket of religion at all. They may feel that religion is either a burden or just something that will cause difficulty. But their spiritual path—and their children's—is usually not so clear.

Without a formal religion, a family can seemingly travel its own route without being restricted by any religious boundaries. If the family is sincere about spirituality, then their child may very well be open-minded about the nature of God. Parents can easily encourage their child to find God in any way that seems appropriate. Above all, these interfaith parents can live by what they deem best for their child, rather than living according to an established doctrine. They can prioritize independence when it comes to matters of belief.

But such a family must also encounter a spiritual

trade-off. Children may feel like outsiders with neighbors and with youngsters who do embrace religion. Older children in particular may be undirected, set off on a search for explicit spiritual values without any religious guidance to depend upon. "Why is it wrong to lie?" a youngster may wonder, but have no doctrine to refer to. Lastly, the family may suffer from a sense of something "missing," without a vehicle for seeking a restorative spiritual community.

Helen, age thirty-seven, is a Catholic woman who is married to a Baptist. The couple has two children who are being reared without any religion. "Well, it's been good for the kids to not have to deal with so much guilt and so much structure that you get with religion. The freedom is really important. My kids probably ask more questions than kids who are brought up Catholic. Certainly more than I did. (Pause.) But every once in a while, especially around the holidays, things feel a little empty. I miss the celebration with a lot of people. I wouldn't wish that my kids could go to church, but I wish there were more families like us to be with."

Regardless of what approach you take as an interfaith couple, I can offer a few recommendations concerning the religion you present to your child. Sort out with each other what specific religious ideas, if any, you want to advocate even before you have children. In that way, future misunderstandings and hurt feelings between you and your spouse can be kept to a minimum.

Your child should be exposed to at least a summary account of both of your religions, even if one or neither religion is observed. A child is entitled to know about family background. Attending a religious service, particularly during a holiday season, is necessary if you want to give your child a feeling of religious community. Make sure that attention to each of your religions is balanced, and make certain that both of you are involved in each educational experience. Don't, in any case, make your child suffer feelings of guilt or betrayal because of religious differences between you and your spouse.

It is also vital that your child understand your current relationships to your religion of origin. "Why doesn't dad go to synagogue?" a youngster may wonder. "Why is mom giving up chocolate for forty days?" another child may question. It is very helpful to tell your child openly how you feel about your religious origin; explain both your positive and negative feelings about it, along with the choices you have made. Encourage your spouse to do likewise. In that way, your child will better understand you both and get to know a little more about your religious backgrounds, too.

It is essential that you provide for your son or daughter a clear and comprehensible set of values and morals, whether or not those precepts come from a formal religion. Your child must have a set of guidelines when it comes to such commonplace childhood matters as fighting at school, telling you the truth, or keeping a friend's secret. You must be certain that your child learns a set of moral standards, whether or not it is based in religion.

Set a time to discuss with your child the idea of choosing a religion for him or herself. As long as your youngster knows he or she is free to choose, and is aware of that early on, your child can proceed with spiritual learning with a realistic sense of purpose. Always in your child's view will be the culmination of his or her upbringing—your child's own adult choice about religion. So plant the seed for that freedom as soon as you begin communicating with your child about religion.

Remember that your role as an interfaith parent has the same responsibilities as any single-faith parent. No matter what your religion or situation, you must be gentle and understanding, open to your child's questions and doubts about all religious beliefs. And, most importantly, you must not be defensive about your own views.

Let your child know that your family is a crucial part of God's community, even if it is different from other families. Provide your son or daughter with the strength to be religiously different, and the tolerance to get along with people of different religious persuasions. Urge your child to use his or her unique situation to find his or her own spiritual path.

What Can You Say to Your Child About God?

The second priority for an interfaith couple is to determine what to communicate about God, since that husband and wife may have grown up with vastly different images of God. In a sense, all married couples must deal with this dilemma. Every husband and wife, once they become parents, must figure out a way to mesh their very personalized ideas about God and communicate that integrated view to a child.

Let's imagine that your concept of God suggests a very nurturing figure who is concerned with nature and the care of all beings. Perhaps your spouse envisions a powerful figure who represents justice and order. What will you tell your child about what God is like?

Particularly if you have diligently informed your child about your background differences, I would emphasize commonalities when speaking about God. Focus on how your image and your spouse's image of God overlap. Look for what binds you together, while still acknowledging that some differences exist. Your child really needs to feel that there is a single, unitary God that both parents worship or acknowledge.

You might talk about the association of God with goodness, if you both believe that is true. You can say that God is around us all the time, if you share that view. You can describe a God who provides an afterlife for human beings, if that too is a religious tenet you share. Finally, you can talk about what role God has in your family life. If you can agree upon that, your parenting on this topic should proceed quite smoothly.

When you do deal with differences in your ideas about God, be absolutely sure to talk them through with your spouse—before either of you shares your ideas with your child. That's the best way to avoid both alarming surprises or hurtful feelings for either of you and any unnecessary tension or confusion for your child. While you do not want to concentrate upon your differences, you do want to confront them without hesitation by saying something like: "No one is certain what God is precisely like, and we have some ideas that are different too. For example, Daddy is convinced that God is like a man and Mommy thinks God may be a woman. But mostly we agree. We both feel strongly that God has all our best interests in mind and looks after us all." That kind of philosophy and communication to your son or daughter can be quite productive. It can alleviate your child's fear and possible misunderstanding concerning God and your special family situation.

"We talk a lot about what we have in common," claims forty-year-old Brent, a father born of Presbyterian parents who married a devoutly Catholic woman. "We tell our sons that we both believe in Christ and in Christ's Resurrection. How he saved us from our sins. I don't think our lives are really all that different than other people's, except maybe that we're more conscious of things. Sometimes I even forget about how our families are different. My wife, Janet, always says that God loves everybody the same. That's pretty much the main belief we have."

As a couple, you should be able to come together and tell your child what you both believe God is like and what God does. As concerned and knowledgeable parents, you should be ready to listen to your child's ideas and questions about God.

What Pragmatic Concerns Confront the Interfaith Family?

The issues of religious choice and different concepts of God can be a major foundation upon which you build the structure of your family. Without clear and wise mutual decisions in those areas, however, it will be extremely difficult to raise your family without tension. But these decisions, important as they are, also require sound considerations in a number of practical ways. An interfaith family must deal with church or synagogue membership, religious school attendance, and the recognition of religious holidays and rituals.

Church, synagogue, or any religious membership will have a great impact in terms of the people who your child meets and your child's own attitude about formal religion. So don't make that choice casually. It's best to discuss it even before you're married. If you haven't done that, come to a joint decision as soon as possible and stick to that decision. There is little more difficult for children than to live with an inconsistent or ambivalent family approach to religion. Whether or not you attend one kind of religious service or another, your preference must correspond to your overall philosophy of religion. For example, if you decide to embrace two religions, your service attendance should include time at both houses of worship.

Of course, you can elect to make religious service attendance optional for your older child. But if you do that, you have to be careful not to create a competitive situation in terms of your respective religious backgrounds. If your child does elect to attend one house of worship over the other, it should be with the explicit approval and understanding of both parents.

The same is true for religious school attendance. Many parents, including many interfaith parents, elect to teach their children about religion themselves. But if you prefer to send your child to religious school, then be sure to follow a similar path for all your children and have each begin at the same age.

Even if you and your spouse decide not to make formal religion an everyday part of your lives, you can still discuss which holidays and rituals you will observe or celebrate. This issue will mostly arise at Christmas and Hanukkah, Passover and Lent and Easter.

"The holidays were always a funny time," says twenty-two-year-old Wendy, a child of Jewish and Catholic parents. "We always celebrated Christmas and Hanukkah, but Hanukkah always got kind of dwarfed by Christmas. We were never sure what we were supposed to believe. My brother, who's twenty-six now, used to say that we changed what we did every year. One year a big tree and lights all over the lawn, the next year just stockings and a menorah. It was pretty confusing sometimes."

As Wendy illustrates, some interfaith families find it difficult to balance and provide equal time for all religious practices. But a life without any religious holidays and celebrations can be very bland, so don't give them up without a lot of forethought. If you decide *not* to celebrate certain (or any) holidays, do so because you have a solid reason, not because it is inconvenient.

Many families, both single-faith and interfaith, celebrate some of the community and cultural aspects of holidays without adhering to all of the related religious tenets. Whatever you decide, see that your youngster knows why you celebrate the holidays that you do. Explain why you commemorate certain holidays and not others, and even tell your child a little bit about the holidays you do not celebrate. For example, why is it that you enthusiastically celebrate Christmas but do not observe Lent? Why won't your child be bar or bat mitzvahed? Spell out the thinking behind your religious choices.

For each holiday and major ritual that you embrace, summarize the religious significance for your child in the course of your conversations. Always remember to point out which religious heritage, mother's or father's, the practice represents. Each parent should also say how he or she feels about the practice. For instance, a parent of Jewish background might explain to his or her child about Christmas: "I didn't grow up with Christmas in my family, but I like it very much because it's fun and it brings people closer together. That's why I enjoy getting involved in the Christmas spirit."

In addition to these items, tell your child openly how your current holiday and worship practices are similar to or different from those that you had when you were a child. What does your interfaith family do that your childhood family did not, and vice versa? Discussing the differences should help your son or daughter understand you both better and will also give them a greater sense of their own heritage.

Since holidays and religious rituals are so much a part of popular culture, your child will be sure to have a lot to say about them. Listen closely to his or her sentiments and preferences. Ask for feedback before and after religious holidays. What does your youngster like about the way you celebrate (or don't) specific holidays and rituals? What doesn't he or she like? How do your family practices differ from his or her friends?

Of course you probably won't do everything your child recommends, but you should take your child's feelings into account.

What About Relatives and Outside Opinion?

The special circumstances of the interfaith family make consideration of religious ideas and practices a particularly complex issue. Growing up with parents of different religious backgrounds, or perhaps with parents who still have divergent views, a child must also deal with a variety of situations that can be obstructive or perplexing. For example, the child must be prepared to deal with the attitudes and responses of family, friends, and neighbors toward him or her. It is the duty of good parents to provide that preparation. Parents must discuss with their children how to react to questions and comments about their mixed religious heritage.

The grandparent-grandchild relationship is always especially important, and your efforts to foster that relationship must be two-directional. Explain to your child that your parents and in-laws are committed to their own backgrounds and religious practices, but that has nothing to do with their love for their grandchild.

Explain to your parents or in-laws that you are attempting to instill respect for their heritage and/or religion in your child, but that you also wish to teach your own ideas and to allow your child to think freely. Ask grandparents to try not to compete with you or other relatives when it comes to religious views. However, I would recommend that you urge grandparents to teach your child about their tradition and way of life, in a nonproselytizing manner.

You might say to a grandparent, "We would really like you to tell Billy and Linda about your religious beliefs so that they can learn about them and know you better. Please don't try to convert them, though, because I want my children to choose religious beliefs independently—without outside pressures. I know that you don't want to place unnecessary weight on their spiritual development."

Terry, a thirty-three-year-old father born into an Assembly of God family and married to a Lutheran woman, recounts how he has dealt with grandparent involvement. "My parents were pretty zealous at first and they would talk to my daughter at length about their views and how they are the path to God. I had to cool them off. I just asked them not to preach so much and just spend time with Jennifer. Since then, they've been fine. They've added a different dimension to our lives."

Your child will also come across any number of situations where a nonfamily member will be curious about interfaith families. Other boys and girls at school may be especially interested, since the idea of two religions in one family may be new to them. Teachers and other adults may also offer a comment or two to your child. While most children and adults will be well-meaning, that may not be the case with everyone. Prepare your child for many possibilities, even a worst case scenario where another child might ridicule your child for being different.

You might teach your child to say to a person who is being sarcastic or somewhat prejudiced: "We believe in our ideas, and nobody has the right to put down another person's beliefs just because they are different. You should change your attitude." In the rare circumstance of a child who is grossly prejudiced or rude, encourage your youngster to refuse to pursue the conversation. Then urge your child to walk away and feel good about himself or herself. Tell your youngster to remember that a person who defends himself or herself with belief, neither backing down nor fighting back, walks with God, who reflects all religious beliefs.

A frequent but difficult family experience for any child is a disagreement between mother and father. Keep in mind that children of interfaith families, aware of their unique family circumstances, may be particularly sensitive to tension.

Now you and your spouse can speak with your child candidly and directly. By the age of seven or eight, children can usually understand that as individuals you have different views. You should explain that as parents you may not always agree, but you still love each other and your child a great deal. You can calmly explain what you disagree about. If you have reached a consensus, say so. If you haven't, you can tell your child that both of you are still working on it. Concerning a sensitive topic, such as whether to go to church or synagogue, only speak to your child when both of you are present. That strategy will protect against your child's possible fear that he or she must decide between the two of you. You must never make your child feel the need to arbitrate between you; that would be painful and unfair. As your youngster grows up, he or she will then be able to make independent choices. Meanwhile, your task is to enrich, not determine, your child's spiritual life and not make it more complicated than it needs to be.

Timmy, a ten-year-old Catholic child brought up by parents from Catholic and Protestant backgrounds, offers an interesting perspective on parental discord in the interfaith family. "When I was little, I would sometimes hear them arguing in their room. Once in a while, it was about church and stuff. I used to wonder what was going on. Then one day I asked them about it. I made them talk to me about it. I liked it that way better. My parents don't fight much any more, so I guess I helped."

Timmy's point of view suggests that parents need to learn from their children, a maxim that can certainly apply to the interfaith family. The challenge for an interfaith family is to learn from each other and to remain open to the continuing lessons brought about by their unique family situation.

Living the Interfaith Life

In the course of everyday life, the interfaith parent and child run into all types of circumstances that are peculiar to their lifestyle. It is difficult to predict the future for any family, but we can generalize about some common situations that interfaith families face. Along with the observations that we have already discussed, there are other specific tips that parents of different religions may wish to discuss with each other.

Tips for Interfaith Parents

1. Be careful not to provide a cloudy or ill-defined set of moral values. Be specific and unequivocally clear about what you believe.
2. Do you think that God has a special purpose in bringing you together as a couple? If so, be candid about what that purpose is. Tell your child explicitly about your reasons for being together. For example, you might say to your child: "God helped us find each other so that we could have you, and also so that we could bring together people of different religions."
3. Seek out other interfaith couples and compare your experiences. What do you have in common? How are you different?
4. Set aside at least one "family hour" per week to discuss

the interfaith experience with your child. Take field trips to a Jewish museum, Christmas concerts, etc.

5. Ask your child what religion he or she will be when your child is your present age. Find out the basis for that choice, because that may be an indication of your child's present view of religion.

6. Discuss with your spouse the possibility that God has no religion. Consider discussing that with your child.

7. Seek out open-minded clergy, and find out more about the ecumenical movements within formal religions. Try to collect such information and make it available to your child.

8. Refresh your own memory for the reasons behind major beliefs and rituals in your tradition, even if you choose not to adhere to them. That way you will be well-equipped to explain things to your child.

9. Invite both sets of grandparents over for dinner if possible. Encourage everyone to talk freely about their backgrounds. A collective dinner can help your child integrate the ideas of both families and traditions.

10. If one parent is Catholic, try to arrange for your child to attend a first communion or a confirmation.

11. If one parent is Jewish, try to arrange for your child to attend a bar mitzvah or bat mitzvah.

12. Depending on your backgrounds and your child's age, discuss the principles of baptism and circumcision.

13. Even if you both come from Western religious backgrounds, acquaint your child with the basic ideas of some Eastern religions, such as Hinduism or Buddhism.

14. Consider how marrying your spouse has changed your

image of God. Do you notice any traces of your spouse's religious background in your image?

15. Always keep in mind the special advantages of having a family that combines two interesting cultures.

16. Apply your situation to the importance of religious beliefs. Let it allow you and your child to take God more seriously than you might otherwise.

17. If you hold different views on the question of the Messiah, state those openly to your child. Either parent should be able to articulate the basis of the other parent's beliefs. For example, a parent of Jewish background should be able to say: "Jesus was a Jewish person who lived about two thousand years ago. Some people believe he had a unique spiritual mission as the son of God. That is not exactly what I believe, though I do believe there will be such a Messiah someday."

18. With relation to afterlife, once again articulate what you believe and what your spouse believes. Mention other possibilities as well. Tell your child no one is certain. If your child is approaching adolescence, be sure to probe for questions and fears. With younger children, keep your description of differences, if you have them, quite simple. Be prepared to answer any question about whether mommy and daddy will go to the same place after they die. Make certain your child does not worry that children go to a different place, precisely because the family has two religions.

19. Keep a record or daily diary of joint decisions you and your spouse make about your child's religious socialization. It will help you to see how your joint views have changed over time, and perhaps where they are heading as well. Try to see how two people come together

as one for the purpose of worshipping a single God and how they decided to raise a son or daughter in the spirit of God.

Ultimately, I hope that all couples will focus on the most crucial element in interfaith parenting. You and your spouse must believe in your compatibility and in your harmony with God. And you should convey these ideas to your child. There is nothing more reassuring for an interfaith child than a solid and meaningful parental relationship. The love and kinship of family life can provide great strength and serve as a buffer for a child against misunderstanding in the world. The respect that you have for each other should nurture similar strength in your child when he or she becomes an adult.

You can then be confident that your tasks have been accomplished with considerable foresight and care. You can be proud of your child and proud of yourself too. You have taken to heart the challenge of creating an interfaith family and beautifully drawn from your own spiritual self to realize that goal.

✑ 10

God's Role in the Life of Your Child

"It's all woven together. All of our lives. And God is at the center.

Tamara
(age 12)"
FROM *THE CHILDREN'S GOD*

Throughout your conversations with your child, you will discover that the panorama of images and ideas about God that you can discuss are endless. In the terms that we often associate with God, the spiritual awareness that can develop in your child is infinite—it can grow as deep as his or her imagination. Because there are so many possibilities, you should always keep in mind a few essential ideas. Remember to concentrate upon God's role in the life of your child, in your child's silent moments as well as his or her episodes of animated conversation. That means taking stock of your child's key spiritual issues. Here is a list of fifteen questions that children commonly ask about God. As you talk to your child, keep in mind that his or her quess are of great concern and your answers will be taken very seriously.

Fifteen Common Questions That Children Ask About God

1. What does God look like?
2. Where does God live?
3. Is God a person? Is he a man or a woman?
4. What does God have to do with a person's death?
5. Does God hear you when you pray?
6. Does God love me?
7. Is everyone the same to God?
8. How can you tell if God is around?
9. Why does God allow war to happen?
10. How is God involved when a kid is born?
11. Can God do everything? What can God do for me? (How can God help me?)
12. Can God do anything at all? (How much power does God have?)
13. How can you get to know God better?
14. Does God still do miracles?
15. Are my mom and my dad always right about God? (Is my minister [or rabbi] always right?)

Focus on what really matters to your child. Don't talk at length about the sky and the stars if they don't fascinate your child. If he or she is intrigued by what God looks like, or even by what God wears, make those themes the center of your conversations. Listen with what some people call a third ear, a knowing sense of what attracts and moves your child, or what distresses him or her.

Do the best you can to help your child answer both easy and difficult questions about God. Most of the time, the answers will have to come from your youngster. Even if you provide a temporary answer, an enduring resolution will emerge as your child grows up. You can assume that God will help your child on the way. Trust in yourself and trust in God, and be sure that you can trust in your child.

Encourage your child to express his or her feelings about God. Doing that can be an enormous asset in trying to come to terms with God's role in our lives. Many children are too inhibited to express their ideas about religion and God. They need to be set free and given the okay to say whatever is on their minds. Don't shackle your child's belief by saying: "It's wrong to believe that." Do not be overly reserved or noncommittal about what your child has to say about God, even if it seems trivial at first. Tell your child, through your words *and* actions, that you genuinely want to know what he or she thinks. You will quickly realize that what initially seems minor may help you get closer to your child—e.g., the olive branch in your child's portrait of God may in fact symbolize your youngster's wish for greater family harmony.

God's role will be further clarified if you try to teach your child about formal religion or about its absence. As we have mentioned, you can describe the details and intricacies of your own beliefs, as well as those of other religions. You can also make certain that your child's notions about religion will not be rigidly ingrained. One way to do that is by discussing beliefs that are far different from yours. But whatever you say about religions, the essential ingredient in your success in guiding your child will be *your* attitude about religion—yours *and* others'. That, along with your spouse's, will determine to a great extent the level of your child's concern and interest. Be open, question constantly, and there is an excellent chance your child will do likewise.

Theoretical concepts of God, such as the Christian notion of the Trinity (see p. 162), or the concept of God sending angels as messengers, are best dealt with by being creative and practical in relating God to your child. As a general principle, it is always a benefit if you discover a new or clever way of communicating to your child. Whether it's a game, a story, a field trip to a religious site or a simple analogy about a household item, the creative hands-on experience will likely be most memorable to your child. In addition, your creative energy is a reflection of your level of interest and involvement.

Invariably, keeping your eyes on one goal, the experience of God as an everyday presence in your child's life, will naturally accomplish these others and make God emotionally and personally meaningful. The idea of God will have very little meaning unless it touches your child in a very direct and intimate way. All parents need to ask the pivotal questions. (How does my child perceive God? Is God comforting or distant?)

Parents must also answer these questions, as complex as they may be. In your responses, you will find the clues to easier communication with your child—not to mention a greater understanding of your own beliefs and purposes as a parent; for your child sees God through you. This is a theme that all parents need to recognize on a daily basis.

Your child needs to feel the love and support of you and of God. For most children, parental involvement is the ultimate way to develop spiritually and to feel good about themselves. Talk with your child face-to-face, not with condescension or distance. You should laugh and play with your child when discussing religion as well as other aspects of his or her life. And be there for serious talks too, because that is what parents are for. Teach your child about a God who is versatile too—a Being that is a Parent to all of us.

Be sure that you include "everyday" situations when you discuss how God participates in our lives so that the concept can be meaningful to your child. God is to be found in songs, laughter, play, work, hurts, celebrations, and so on. Most important, no matter what your religion or your child's may be, God is at work in your child's life, and he or she should have a sense of that.

Please recall that children, including your youngster, need substantial direction; considerable guidance is necessary for them to follow a healthy path. Be prepared to offer structured parenting when it is called for. Consider your own life experiences and be ready to show your child possible ways to greater fulfillment. And help your child embrace a God who offers direction and delivers a person from confusion and uncertainty. This will strengthen your child's faith.

Notice that many children need a parent or God to act as a sounding board, even if that means feeling like a target every once in a while. Perhaps your youngster needs you in this way. Full of troublesome or just lively feelings, your child may need to unwind or release his or her emotions in order to see the world clearly. You may need to be there to listen and to absorb the weight of your child's experiences. You can be the dependable confidant who is privy to the ups and downs of childhood, as seen through the eyes of your son or daughter. Introduce your child to a God who is a good listener too. You might even teach your child to pray by suggesting a favorite prayer or by asking your child to select his or her own.

Consider that a few children do not seem to need their parents that much. Independent souls, these children are surprisingly well-adjusted without discernible parental involvement. Is your child like that? Perhaps, then, all that is required is that you respect your child's interests, assertiveness, and spirit. If your child is a natural explorer of spirituality and the world at large, you can check in to see how things are going. Let your child know about a God who allows people their freedom and yet continues to care for them, and tell him that you can see the God in him. That is pertinent advice for all parents.

The key to spiritual parenting is being sensitive to the nuances of your child's personality and individual curiosities and needs. Perfect sensitivity may be impossible, for that is a quality particular to God alone. But you are very capable of being an outstanding parent—and that will be more than sufficient for the development of your child's spirit and zest for life.

I hope that as you finish this book and begin conversations with your son or daughter, it will be with a reasonable idea of how to discuss the notion of God. Fortunately, you can always look for God in two different manifestations, both of whom have God within them. These expressions of God are you and your child.

Your child and God—it is a natural combination of person and spirituality. Children embody a beautiful sense of innocence and goodness. Because of their youth and vitality, and their wide open eyes, they remind adults of faith and optimism.

As you have undoubtedly noted about your youngster, children have a special spirit about them, and just when a parent or teacher least expects it, they will volunteer to share this spirit with you. More often than not, they'll tell you just how they see the world. They'll even spontaneously comment about God with refreshing honesty.

"About those diseases, Mr. God . . ." more than one brave youngster has said. "Thanks for all the beautiful rivers and toads and frogs," some other children comment. "I wish I could see You so that I could draw You better," another child poignantly offers. For children, no one is too far away for conversation, and that includes God.

It is your child's wonderful spirit that you should keep in mind as you think about God. Watch how that spirit endures as your child grows. That spirit is a reminder to you of your own spirit and of the God in you. It is your challenge—as a parent and as a person—to locate that spirit and cultivate its growth.

Just as your child already is developing an inner sense of God, so is there a divine spirit in you. Your parental journey is very much concerned with that spirit and this book is an attempt to kindle it. Your inner spirit inspires you to love and cherish your child and to give of yourself freely. It will lead you to encourage your youngster to be the best he or she can be. You can trust in that inner spirit.

Parenting is both an unparalleled responsibility and a boundless joy—and it is clearly a spiritual journey not to be missed. Accepting parenthood means accepting life, and you are currently engaged in passing on God—the giver of life—to your child.

Whatever your concept of God, huge or small, black or white, male or female, it is you who will largely determine not only the kind of person your child will be, but also the kind of God your child will embrace. When all the possible relationships in the world are considered, there is no greater opportunity than this—introducing your child to God—for any parent to make a lasting and significant contribution to the world.

A

Abortion, 165
Abraham, 128, 145–47
Adam, 93, 97–100, 154
Afterlife, 34, 39–40, 170
Age Differences. *See* Children
Agnosticism, 139–41
Allah, 132–33
Andrew, 135
Angels, 76, 204
Anglican Church, 170–71
Ascension Thursday, 165
Ash Wednesday, 165
Atheism, 140–41

B

Baptists, 63, 169–70
Bar Mitzvah, 69, 155, 192
Bat Mitzvah, 155
Bible, The Holy, 17, 25, 27, 29, 32,
    61, 69, 73–74, 97, 100–01,
    123, 140, 145–48, 176
Birth, 57, 99, 202
Book of Common Prayer, 171
Book of Discipline, 168

Book of Hymns, 168
Buddha, 128
Buddhism, 133–35

C

Catholicism, 124, 136–38, 143,
    155–65, 173, 179, 180–81
Childhood and Society, 16
Children
    Catholic, 155–65
    curiosities, 3–10
    development of, 6–31
    drawings of God, 87–90
    gender differences,
        boys, 84–85
        girls, 85–86
    getting started with, 55–70
    God's role in the life of, 201–08
    home life, 11–31
    ideas about birth, 57, 99
    ideas about death, 40–41
    interests by age
        4- to 6-year-olds, 19, 27,
            62–64, 97, 104
        7- to 9-year-olds, 19–20,
            27–28, 64–66, 97, 104

10- to 12-year-olds, 20, 28, 35, 66–67, 104
interfaith, 180–200
Jewish, 144–55
letters to God, 11, 32, 55, 93, 142
media influences on, 29, 75
notions of God, 71–92
personality differences, 77–83
Protestant, 165–74
questions they ask, 202
relation to parents, 3–10, 201–08
relation to pets, 116
schools for, 56, 123, 174
The Children's God, 201
Christianity, 63, 69, 124, 131, 132, 147, 152, 155–79, 184
Christmas, 57, 69, 98, 135, 142, 155, 156, 160, 161, 163–64, 192–93
Church, 160–65
Cosmology, 122
Crucifixion, 87–90, 136, 169

D

David, 72, 73, 145, 148
Dawidowicz, Lucy, 153
Dear God, 11, 32, 93, 142, 180
Death, 38, 40–41, 202
Divorce, 136, 161–62

E

Easter, 155, 156, 160
Eastern Orthodox, 135–36
Eban, Abba, 153
Egyptians, 124
Elijah, 128
Episcopalians, 170–71
Erikson, Erik, 16–17

Eve, 93, 97, 98–100, 154
Exodus, Book of, 73, 100

F

Family
atmosphere, 11–31
Catholic, 155–65
conversations, 70
God's manifestations in, 114–15
God's role in, 201–08
interfaith, 180–200
Jewish, 144–55
Protestant, 165–74
representation in the God image, 71–80
roles, 6–10
values, 3–10, 201–08
Flood, in Noah's time, 154
Free Will, 173–74

G

Gandhi, 132
Gender Differences of Children, see Children
Genesis, Book of, 99, 154
God
anger toward, 48–50
Creator, 97–100
doubt and questioning of, 9–10, 33–36, 44–46, 64–66, 70, 95–96, 141, 179
faith in, 9, 17–18, 33–43, 58–60, 64–66, 96, 141, 179
fear of, 47–48, 65, 93
grandparent images of, 79
guilt toward, 50–52
images of, 22, 33–35, 41–43, 46–52, 58, 67, 71–92
loving, 12–15

maternal images of, 78
mystery of, 94–97
paternal images of, 77–78
relation to nature, 106–11
relation to science, 106–09
relation to sexuality and love,
    112–14
role in the world, 93–117
war and peace and, 100–04
Gospels, 156

H

Hell, 170
Henry VIII, 171
Highway to Heaven, 65
Hinduism, 128, 130–32
Holidays, 19–20, 56, 69, 115, 155,
    187, 191–93
Holocaust, 145, 152–54, 155
The Holy Spirit, 157, 162–63

I

I Ching, 32
Immaculate Conception, 136, 137
Inherit the Wind, 108
Interfaith Couples, 180–200
Isaac, 145, 150
Islam, 128, 132–33

J

Jacob, 65–66, 145
James, 135
Jesus, 23, 61, 72, 89–90, 128,
    135–36, 155–58, 162–63,
    168, 176, 178, 184, 199
Job, 151
John the Baptist, 29
Joseph, 29, 74, 145, 150–51

Judaism, 63, 101, 124, 128, 132,
    143, 144–55, 179, 180–81
Jung, Carl, 46

K

Know Yourself Inventory, 33–35
Koran, 32, 132
Kosher, 147

L

Lent, 165, 191
Love, in the context of religion,
    12–15, 112–14
Luther, Martin, 166, 167
Lutherans, 63, 167–68

M

Mark, 135
Marriage, 69, 161–62, 165
Mary, 165
Mass, 157–58
The Meaning and End of Religion,
    37
Media Depictions of Religion, 29,
    75
Messiah, 155, 199
Methodists, 168–69
Miracle on 34th Street, 70
Miracles, 202
Mitzvot, 146
Mohammed, 132
Mormons, 136–38
Moses, 29, 30, 72, 145–48, 176
Mother Theresa, 164

N

Nature, 106–11
Ninety-Five Theses, 166

Nirvana, 134
Nuns, 160, 163

O

Original Sin, 99

P

Parables, 156
Parental
    anger toward God, 48–50
    beliefs, 37–43
    Catholic, 155–65
    conversations with children,
        55–70
    doubts, 44–46
    fears, 47–48
    freedoms, 20–31
    guidance, 7–10
    guilt, 50–52
    interfaith, 180–200
    involvement, 26–31
    Jewish, 144–55
    love, 12–15
    Protestant, 165–74
    response to child's curiosity,
        3–10
    responsibilities, 3–31
    role, 6–8
    self-knowledge, 32–52
    trust, 15–20
Passover, 149, 151
Piaget, Jean, 99
Personality, in the God figure,
        77–83
    The Angry Villain, 82
    The Distant Thing in the Sky,
        81
    The Friendly Ghost, 80
    The Inconsistent God, 81
    The Lover in Heaven, 81

The Once and Future God, 82
    The Therapist (Dr. God), 82–83
Peter, 135
Pets, 116
The Pope, 157, 161, 164, 166
    infallibility, 157
Prayer, 68, 71, 202
Presbyterians, 169, 172
Priests, 162–65
Protestantism, 124, 136, 138, 143,
        165–74, 182, 183
Purgatory, 158–59
Puritans, 169
Puja, 131

Q

Quakers, 138–39
Queries, 139

R

Reformation, 166–68
Religion, General. *See also*
        Catholicism, Judaism,
        Protestantism
    curiosity about, 3–10, 22
    formal, 13, 28, 39, 41, 65, 68,
        72–73, 143–44, 175
    meaning of, 4–5, 10
    nature and purpose, 121–41
    schools, 56, 123, 174, 190, 191
Resurrection, 165, 169
Rosh Hashanah, 69, 148–49

S

Sabbath, 146–47
Satan, 159
Saul, 151
Schism, 166

Science, 106–09
Separatists, 169
Sexuality, 112–14
Shi'ah, 133
Siddhartha, 134
Smith, Joseph, 136–37
Smith, Wilfred Cantwell, 37
Solomon, 150
Spirituality
    atmosphere, 11–31
    development, 6–10
    freedom, 20–26
    guidance, 7–10
    involvement, 26–31
    love, 12–15
    trust, 15–20
Sunni, 133
Sutras, 134

T

Torah, 148
The Trinity, 136, 156–57,
    161–63, 168
Tzedakah, 146

U

Unaffiliated Belief, 175–79
Unitarians, 172

V

The Veda, 130

W

Weddings, 69
Wesley, Charles, 168
Wesley, John, 168
Wiesel, Elie, 153

Y

Yom Kippur, 148–49, 155
Young, Brigham, 137

Z

Zen Buddhism, 134

ABOUT THE AUTHOR

DAVID HELLER, Ph.D., is the author of fifteen books, including *Dear God: Children's Letters to God, Love Is Like a Crayon Because It Comes in All Colors* and *My Mother Is the Best Gift I Ever Got.* Additional books include: *The Best Christmas Presents Are Wrapped in Heaven* and *Just Build the Ark and the Animals Will Come: Children on Bible Stories.*

Dr. Heller graduated summa cum laude from Harvard and received his doctorate from the University of Michigan. His work has been featured on *20/20* and in *Parents Magazine, People, Parenting, Cosmopolitan, Good Housekeeping, Catholic Digest, Woman's Day, Redbook, New Woman* and many other periodicals. His books have been translated into ten different languages.

Dr. Heller lives in Boston with his wife and collaborator, Elizabeth.